Advance Praise for *Scratching River*

Michelle Porter's *Scratching River* is a stunning and ruminative poetic work of creative non-fiction that moves across time, geography, Métis history, and kinship. Porter honours her Métis family and ancestors through past, present, and future poetics. The interwoven narratives wrap around Porter's mother, Porter's own story as a daughter and sister, and her relationship with her older brother, who was diagnosed as schizophrenic and autistic, and abused in a rural Alberta group home. *Scratching River* illustrates the powerful journey of reconciliation, as Porter's family reconnects amongst their ongoing movement and relocation to find their way back to the river they share.

—Shannon Webb-Campbell, author of *Lunar Tides* and
I Am a Body of Land

In a single sentence, Michelle Porter lets us see her big brother and the river as one—the heart of the telling, tortured, forever in motion, compelling us to follow. This unity, swiftly as it is achieved, is the result of a life spent not just seeing but feeling everything on earth as part of a single being. This is a book of voices: human, animal, water, land, past, present, singing. This is a story of hard truths courageously told. We need it.

—Richard Harrison, Governor General's Award-winning
author of *On Not Losing My Father's Ashes in the Flood*
and *Hockey Poems*

Gnarled and knotted, *Scratching River* is a bricolage of intimate memories, newspaper articles, investigative reports, a century-old memoir, and practical knowledge. It meanders and flows like an old river, burbling and rushing into a story of past and present, human and environment, colonialism and violence, justice, and love.

—Sonja Boon, author of *What the Oceans Remember*

Like her astonishing brother does in this book, Michelle Porter takes me by the hand and runs with me into a new world. I have never been here before. The sad and heroic stories which she braids together flood my heart and stretch my soul. I love this book.

—Andy Jones (CM), actor and writer

This is a book on the move. It eddies through still-water ponds and tumbles over cataracts; it branches into ox-bows and branches again. One moment it speaks so quietly in your ear, and another, it breaks you apart. *Scratching River* is a wise and necessary work in these times in which we strive for reconciliation around contested readings of those words "home" and "land." Braiding together varied voices and forms of attention into a deeply personal inquiry into place and belonging, Michelle Porter is making some of the most innovative and compelling creative non-fiction today. *Scratching River* is a magnificent achievement.

—Robert Finley, Memorial University of Newfoundland and Labrador Creative Writing Program

This book is a kind of prayer, a "map in words" that navigates the treacherous, uncharted territory of our collective souls—a necessary exploration if we are ever to land safely, solidly, truthfully, on future shores. A triumph, *Scratching River* is proof that the healing power of narrative is a gift a writer can transmit to readers.

—Sheree Fitch, author of *You Won't Always be This Sad* and *Kiss the Joy as it Flies*

Michelle Porter's *Scratching River* is both a reckoning and an elegy; a scathing, powerful roar against social injustice, the scars of trauma, climate crisis, environmental damage and, at the very same time, a love song to the power of family, Métis history, rivers, Bison, burdock, and the Métis storyteller and musician, Louis Goulet, who is her great-great-grandfather's brother. Porter artfully braids together a portrait of her brother, Brendon Porter, who was horrifically brutalized in an institution for mentally disabled adults, with a rich understanding of the lives and habits of rivers, grassland, bison, and the threatened ecosystems of the prairies, to profound effect. Here also are wisdom and tenderness, stories full of dancing, hunting, travelling by ox-drawn cart or Greyhound bus, and sleeping under the stars. Porter roves gracefully through the past, present, and future and proves herself a consummate writer for our times. *Scratching River* is a rare gift.

—Lisa Moore, author of *This Is How We Love*

Scratching River

Life Writing Series

Wilfrid Laurier University Press's Life Writing series celebrates life writing as both genre and critical practice. As a home for innovative scholarship in theory and critical practice, the series embraces a range of theoretical and methodological approaches, from literary criticism and theory to autoethnography and beyond, and encourages intersectional approaches attentive to the complex interrelationships between gender, class, race, ethnicity, sexuality, ability, and more. In its commitment to life writing as genre, the series incorporates a range of life writing practices and welcomes creative scholarship and hybrid forms. The Life Writing series recognizes the diversity of languages, and the effects of such languages on life writing practices within the Canadian context, including the languages of migration and translation. As such, the series invites contributions from voices and communities who have been under- or misrepresented in scholarly work.

Series editors

Sonja Boon, Memorial University of Newfoundland
Marlene Kadar, York University

Scratching River

River

MICHELLE PORTER

WILFRID LAURIER
UNIVERSITY PRESS

Wilfrid Laurier University Press acknowledges the support of the Canada Council for the Arts for our publishing program. We acknowledge the financial support of the Government of Canada through the Canada Book Fund for our publishing activities. Funding provided by the Government of Ontario and the Ontario Arts Council. This work was supported by the Research Support Fund.

Library and Archives Canada Cataloguing in Publication

Title: Scratching river / Michelle Porter.
Names: Porter, Michelle (Poet), author.
Series: Life writing series.
Description: Series statement: Life writing series
Identifiers: Canadiana (print) 20210286385 | Canadiana (ebook) 20210286911 | ISBN 9781771125444 (softcover) | ISBN 9781771125451 (EPUB) | ISBN 9781771125468 (PDF)
Subjects: LCSH: Porter, Michelle (Poet) | LCSH: Porter, Michelle (Poet)—Family. | LCSH: Métis—Prairie Provinces—Biography. | LCSH: Métis—Prairie Provinces—History. | LCSH: Schizophrenics—Care—Prairie Provinces. | LCSH: Schizophrenics—Family relationships—Prairie Provinces. | LCSH: Autistic people—Care—Prairie Provinces. | LCSH: Autistic people—Family relationships—Prairie Provinces. | CSH: Authors, Canadian (English)—Prairie Provinces—Biography. | LCGFT: Autobiographies. | LCGFT: Biographies.
Classification: LCC PS8631.O7374 A3 2022 | DDC C818/.603—dc23

Cover design by Lime Design Inc.
Interior design by Daiva Villa.
Front cover image by salajean, Shutterstock.com
Copy Editor: Rhonda Kronyk

© 2022 Wilfrid Laurier University Press
Waterloo, Ontario, Canada
www.wlupress.wlu.ca

This book is printed on FSC® certified paper. It contains recycled materials and other controlled sources, is processed chlorine free, and is manufactured using biogas energy.
Printed in Canada

Wilfrid Laurier University Press is located on the Haldimand Tract, part of the traditional territories of the Haudenosaunee, Anishinaabe, and Neutral peoples. This land is part of the Dish with One Spoon Treaty between the Haudenosaunee and Anishnaabe peoples and symbolizes the agreement to share, to protect our resources, and not to engage in conflict. We are grateful to the Indigenous peoples who continue to care for and remain interconnected with this land. Through the work we publish in partnership with our authors, we seek to honour our local and larger community relationships, and to engage with the diversity of collective knowledge integral to responsible scholarly and cultural exchange.

Contents

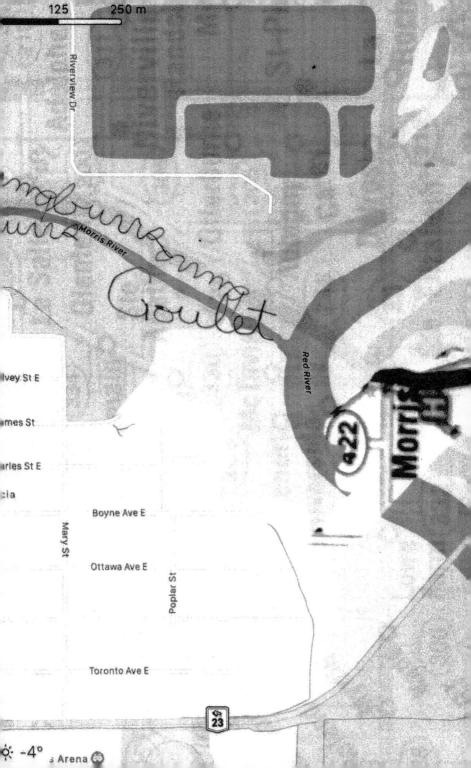

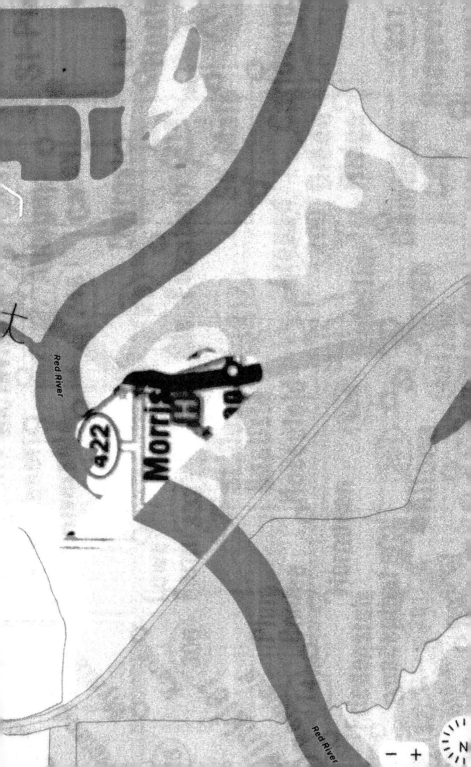

"The Red River trails have provided one of the most intriguing, colorful, and hotly debated chapters in Minnesota's history. Although scholars have dealt thoroughly with the economic and political implications of the trade that moved over the routes, the rutted paths themselves have always been something of a conundrum. They crossed, for the most part, a level, open and well-watered country, and they were not confined by geography to fixed—and therefore easily traceable—routes."

—*The Red River Trails: Oxcart Routes Between St. Paul and the Selkirk Settlement 1820–1870* (pg. v)

St. Albert

Edmonton

Alberta 2

Camrose

Wetaskiwin

**3 hrs. 2 min.
Fastest**

Red Deer

3 hrs. 46 min.

Rumsey
Natural Area

Alberta 2

Airdrie

Calgary

25   50 km

how long?

See can I can hear my on the phone

how long?

burn un

St. Albert
Calgary *hospital*

Now   Plan

Options

Transit Directions Not Available

Transit directions between these locations are not available in Maps.

3 hrs. 11 min.
315 km

monton

Camrose

Wetaskiwin

2 min.
est

RI

ear my mother
he phone

Rumsey
Natural Area

RIEL Riel

RIEL
USINESS
PARK

n unit

CHAPTER ONE

Scratching River

Once, there was a boy who belonged to the prairies. His mother was a Métis woman with dark hair she kept long and permed while her children were young.

The day mom called the hospital in Calgary to find out what had happened to our older brother? Were we living along the Sturgeon River then? Yes? We moved into and out of apartments in those buildings so many times.

When mom called the hospital, I don't know, weren't we in the larger apartment on the second floor? Or were we in the smaller one on the third?

Memory offers up the beige carpets that were in all those apartments. I can hear a phone ringing and I know mom will answer and we will find out about Brendon. But memory is playing tricks. Mom says she called the Ranch, so I couldn't have heard the phone. But I hear ringing. Mom talks to the people at the Ranch, and they tell mom Brendon is in the hospital, but not to worry—he's just fine and will only be in overnight. Don't bother coming down to see him.

Mom called the hospital right after that. Even now, almost thirty years later, my body becomes still and I hold my breath to listen to the memory of my mother's stilted phrases.

Thirty years later, I listen to mama's voice on the phone across the country from where I stand at my kitchen sink, washing dishes as she talks. The memory is still fresh with her, open and unhealed. Oh, God, she says, the horror. She repeats the first two words as if she believes. Oh God, she says again. I rinse a chipped beige bowl imprinted with flower patterns. Then I set it in the drying rack, lean it against the plate with the green border.

Burdock root is right there along all the rivers in the first paragraph of chapter one of the life story of my great-great-grandfather's brother, Louis Goulet. The book is an oral history, a transcription of stories he told to a researcher about his life as a prairie Métis. He was living during a time of "profound change" for the Métis and for all Indigenous Peoples. This was the mid-to-late 1800s, and the buffalo herds were dying out. The hunt and the way of life faltered with the roaming buffalo herds. But our culture didn't. There was the tradition of change. There was the ability to bring your ways of living into a future you were giving to the next generation. That stayed with so many Métis families, was passed on down to us by our relations.

THREE HOMES CLOSED: ASSAULT ALLEGATIONS AT AUTISTIC FACILITIES

Chris Dawson and **Ashley Geddes**. *Calgary Herald;*
Calgary, Alta. 29 Jan 1993: A1/ FRONT.

The province has shut down three group homes for autistic adults in southern Alberta, leaving the owner stunned amid allegations of assault and physical abuse.

"I have been hurt and hurt and hurt, and I'm tired of it," said ███████████, who will meet with a Calgary lawyer this morning with an eye towards possible legal action.

Have you cut open a burdock root? It smells angry, like a couple bickering or a child denied candy at the checkout line.

An Absent River

…leaves a trail. As for my mother she wanted to flow into the old trails, the ones no longer spoken of except in the old stories. If you know the way, you can walk along any of these and find the telling details stitched into layers of earth and the plot layered into the rock. When my brother had to go, mama returned to the banks of these absent rivers again and again.

She had a rope. She tied one end around her leg and one around Brendon's leg. It was an agreement, this nylon connection between them, this sullen umbilical cord, because if she didn't, he'd run. Middle of the day, middle of the night, middle of winter, it didn't matter. Mom liked to tell us how she ran after

Brendon, big and round with the next baby, trying to move fast enough, trying to catch up to her firstborn son. Sometimes she had to call the cops. They knew her. They knew Brendon. Brought him home sometimes before my mom even noticed he was gone.

Reading an Old Riverbed

Some rivers have a lot of small channels that continually split and join. There were five of us, two boys and three girls. Rivers with these kinds of channels are called braided rivers. They split and join and split and join and split off again. Sometimes they curve away for so long, you don't know for a long while that they're part of a larger river. Mama, she was one of seven, three boys and four girls. It was the aunts who brought everyone together, each of us balancing paper plates and sitting on folding chairs in their yards or around tables in their kitchens. No one spoke much about the Red River. It was always the fiddles they talked about. When a channel splits off from the main river, it only joins up again when the land offers an opening, when conditions allow.

Or maybe the burdock root you've sliced in two smells of righteous anger, the fury that rises in reaction to rights denied and land stolen? I can't tell where your anger originates or what it tastes like. Mine is sharp and abrasive, but musty. Following the knife's work, the burdock smells of the day after. The day after what? For me, the day after a battle fought in the forest with guns. It reaches inside of you and lingers there in the grass and the soil.

∞

She knew she had to let Brendon go one day when she was trying to make supper. She was pregnant and she was at her breaking point. I imagine her in this story, trying to peel potatoes or cutting up apples for a pie because she liked to bake back then. She was trying to be a picture from a magazine advertisement then, to create the perfect home and family in an image from someone else's imagination. But she couldn't let Brendon run away again. That's why he was tied to her. He was getting bigger, running faster and farther. Sitting there on the floor at her feet, Brendon was crying, a mournful cry because he just wanted to be on the go. Moving on, moving on, traveling.

The Names of Rivers

Rivers bear so many names in their shifting lives. It took the experts a long time to settle on the blended diagnoses of schizophrenia and autism. My brother didn't fit their idea of what either of those two things were, and he still doesn't, really. The Gratias River where my ancestor Louis was born is called the Morris River, for the municipality that stands there now. It's important to remember that it was once called Scratching River—and that it had other names before then, too.

My big brother taking me by the hand, pulling me into his world. One hand cupping one ear. A big smile. In a sing-song voice: da-da-da, and da-da-da again. Off I went with him.

Here's a telling of a map in words. Here's an oral map of the route they'd have taken, according to Louis when they were travelling from their Red River homes to their hunting grounds and then to their wintering homes and here and there to visit family and relations.

By oxcart from St. Norbert on the Sale River in the direction of Missouri, to the foothills of the first range of the Rocky Mountains, then back to the Red River, meeting it at its junction with the Cheyenne River in North Dakota. From there, north, to give birth to Louis Goulet on October 6, 1859 in Red River country on the banks of the Gratias River and then, after the birth, back to Sale River. For a bit.

Scratching River is a name that considers the gratchias, the burdock that grows thick along the river's banks. It's this stout weed Louis spoke of all those years ago when his memories were recorded. It's a plant you can't forget really. Gratchias grows in wet and mud, and the banks of rivers offer the perfect conditions for the burdock to grow. Gratchias is a name for all those burrs that dig at the river's quick hips, for the stout purple clusters that hook and irritate, born to be tenacious and prickly.

The name Gratias River, or La Rivière aux Gratias, has been dropped from common use. Except in Louis's oral history and a few other sources, the name, the Gratias River, has vanished.

Scratching River is more common a name for that river now. It is a name used in historical descriptions of the earliest Mennonite immigrants and their communities. This name lives with stories about a small group of Mennonites who settled at Scratching River in 1874, not the Gratias River, and, of course, not at the river that went by the name it was called before the Métis knew it.

There is a new plaque at a new park in the municipality of Morris that unfurls the Métis history of the area. In an interview with a journalist, one of Morris's local historians explained the importance of the newly named Charette Park. "A lot of people don't realize that there was a significant Métis population in the area before 1812," said the historian to the reporter with the Winnipeg Free Press.

Installed in 2016, the plaque tells about the Charette family that made a home at that site in the early 1800s. Their small family settled halfway between the Red River Settlement and the Morris River, the plaque says. The mini-history offered on the plaque mentions that the Morris River was formerly Scratching River.

How many times did she ask herself why she chose that home for her oldest son, for my brother, for Brendon? Every day, I think. What went wrong, my mother would say, is that she believed. Hope doesn't always live up to its promises, and hope led my mother down paths that ended in the middle of an unfamiliar woods late at night, no shelter at all, and no water nearby. She always said she thought her boy, her Brendon, was hiding away somewhere and that somebody just had to find the right way to reach him. That was her hope, anyway. She hadn't been able to reach him. And then along comes a person who says she can bring the boy out of his autism, who promises a cure, who offers the kind of breadcrumb hope that leads right into the middle of belief. And mama believed with her whole heart.

In the hand and up close, it's easy to see how the burdock's burr had to have been the inspiration for velcro, as history has it. The burr is intricate. There's a strange, almost alien elegance to its design. There are hundreds of tiny, hooked slivers, the inspiration for some of the most common fastening technology we have today. In the palm, the burr rests so lightly. Yet, there is something stubborn and prickly that resists the closing of the hand, the crushing of the seed in the fist. It is a burr, after all.

1 hr. 34 min.

1 hr. 30 min.
Fastest

Innisfail

Bowden

Olds

Didsbury

Carstairs

Alberta 2

Airdrie

Cochrane

Alberta 201

his childhood school and from home fast food res

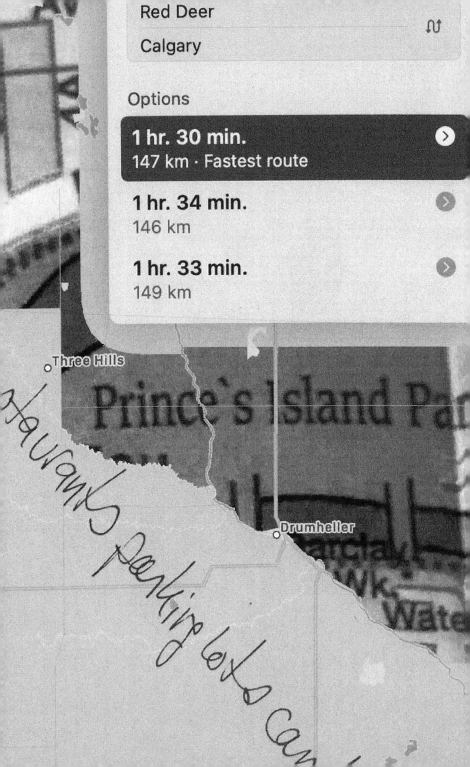

CHAPTER TWO

The West Bank of Red River

The boy's mother was a descendant of the large and open-handed Goulet line from the Red River, reaching back to the days of the buffalo hunt, before Manitoba became part of Canada, before all the aching grassland was turned for crops, before the Red River cart, even.

Ponds Versus Rivers

To remain still or pretty much in place for a while, that is for the pond or the lake. Mama looked at ponds and stood on the edges of lakes, but she always walked away from them. My brother enjoyed walking the long, sinuous hallways in the psychiatric unit of a newly built hospital, became restless in rooms with four walls, with doors that didn't lead anywhere. Rivers are always asking to roam, to go looking for new places.

It is my sister who mentions my brother when we talk on the phone. We're living on opposite ends of the country and between our children and our husbands and our lives we only talk once a month or so. But one day she talks about our brother and the home he went to and the injuries. She's been researching things, she says, looking up old news stories, looking up the owner of that first adult home our brother lived in.

$$\infty$$

We grew up in the backseat of a car, didn't we? Then, we built our home on the highways between the speed limit signs, 100km/hr, and in those little apartments and the cramped houses of time it took to drive to Calgary to see our brother. On those trips I imagined my brother's life was something I could see through the window. In the winter, the windows stayed closed and the heater was on, but we could scratch our brother's name in the frost. His name, Brendon, and all our names, side by side. In the summer we could turn the black plastic handles around and around until the smudged glass was only an inch tall and a cooling wind blew onto our cheeks and our over-heated necks. His river was always on the other side, and though we couldn't always see it we knew it was there. Sometimes we agreed that his river was just over the horizon. Sometimes we decided it was in the ground beneath us, moving among rocks we couldn't see, weaving in and out of the streams of our own trickling selves. And sometimes he was right there beside us, a big muddy river between banks that invited us to put our arms out the windows and wave, to call out in a sing-song chorus, Waa-ter, waaa-ter, waaa-terrrr.

Our only home was there, in the three hours and two minutes between St. Albert and Calgary; in the three hours and five minutes between Spruce Grove and Calgary; in the one hour and thirty minutes between Red Deer and Calgary. And the return. Did the return always seem longer to you than the leaving, somehow? It did to me.

*There Were Things Going on We Knew Nothing About**

NEWS ANCHOR: [Network reporter and producer] have been investigating charges of abuse at the Ranch. Tonight their report on the silent victims and how in spite of years of rumours and horror stories the Alberta government did nothing.

That place there in Calgary, his safe place. The one we visited when we were kids. My big brother taking me by the hand, pulling me into his world. The back yard of the school. The toys, the trees, the swings, the trampoline. The trees. He'd pull branches. One hand cupping one ear. A big smile. In a sing-song voice: da-da-da, and da-da-da again. Off I went with him.

The entire family was camped near two rivers on the return trip from a buffalo hunting expedition when Louis Goulet was born. So, it makes sense that the name of a river is the second word in the book that records Goulet's memories, *Vanishing Spaces*. No accident, that. Louis Goulet and his family made a life along rivers that flowed through land that is part of today's map of Canada. But they weren't in Canada yet, not then.

On their way back from the hunting expedition. They weren't too far from their home and land along the Rivière Sale, upstream a ways from where it empties into the Red. Louis didn't wait until they were back there to come into the world. He wasn't born along the Rivière Sale, a river named

---

*   The sections titled "There Were Things Going on We Knew Nothing About" are direct transcriptions of a CBC investigative documentary about allegations of abuse at the Ranch. My mother was interviewed for the episode and appears in it. It aired on January 27, 1993. Digital copies remain in the archives and can be accessed by contacting an archivist at the news organization that produced the show: CBC "PRIME TIME NEWS AUTISTIC ABUSE–SILENT VICTIMS - 1993-01-27."

for its dirt and the "muddy waters it carried down from the immense, marshy plain that fed its headwaters." Louis was born on The Gratias River, a river they were following on their way back to their little log house. It was a river named for a weed— or an herb, depending on your relationship with the plant.

The Goulet family farm in 1859 was located just off the west bank of the Red River, upstream from the mouth of the Sale River. The Sale River still flows into the Red, but the Goulet farm became the village of Morris. The rivers kept moving on and on and so did the Goulets.

Louis was born on the return from a buffalo hunt. His mother probably rode much of the journey in the back of the Red River Cart, beading and sewing, as the wheels squealed and the horses pulled, and the fetus inside her shed gills, grew a heart, and waited for his own life to flow from the river of his mother and into the moving world.

The plant called burdock appears in the fourth line of *Vanishing Spaces,* the book that gives us the transcription of Louis Goulet's memories: "The Gratias [river] got its name for a type of burdock that grew thick on the banks for the whole length of the river." A few lines later, Louis offers us the Métis name for burdock, gratchias. Louis "came into the world on October 6, 1859" on the banks of this river. Right away you know that the river and the plant are important to his life story. It becomes important even though there isn't another reference to that river or that plant after chapter one. The moving on, the itch and the burr and the riverbed and the open prairie, they're all in the blood and in the root.

For my Métis ancestors back then, farming was most often just a supplement to a buffalo-centred lifestyle. The houses that were built along the rivers become home between journeys. Their familiar structures often marked the beginning or the end of a journey, a story they looked back on as they traveled away and anticipated as they traveled back. The trails and the relations and the places they wintered over, these were homeland as much as the farms and the houses that stood there. So I've been told.

This traveling attachment to home didn't result in the kind of farming the colonies needed.

Farmers who grew crops only for their People weren't dependent on an overseas market for survival. Farmers who worked the land one year and left for the hunt the following year didn't have a lot of surplus crops to sell. But they had everything they needed for themselves, and they sold the meat and hides and pemmican to the settlers, who needed them to survive because who could count on a good crop year?

The colonial powers frowned on the Métis approach to agriculture. Sure, their colonists relied on the buffalo hunt. But they preferred a farmer who stayed on one piece of land all year long, every year, ideally growing so much surplus that they'd make a profit for colonial coffers, though there was nothing left for these farmers the years the hard times came, when the weather didn't cooperate and the crops failed. The missionaries "preached [this kind of] farming as much as gospel," Louis said.

The October he turned eighteen, Brendon aged out of the residential institution for children in Calgary. By then, he'd outgrown the other children, the skinny, frail boys whose eyes saw another world. Do you still hear those boys scream melodies down the hallways and laugh loud and long for reasons we couldn't fathom, and do you remember how this amazed us as children? A few wore helmets and some could speak to us if they wanted. They hardly ever wanted. Our brother vocalized in a sort of wordless sing-song, but communicated only in sign language, with a vocabulary probably no larger than a dozen or so signs. And this is still true now, as he approaches his fifth decade, beautiful tall man without words.

Rivers Can Split and Weave to Cope with Barriers

A deposit of earth can become a temporary island and rise above the flow of a braided river. Then the river splits into channels that flow on either side. It is possible for these channels to continue alone. It is also possible for them to reconnect and cross over as conditions allow.

One of the frontline care workers at the residence and school for autistic children said that they all knew Brendon would make something happen when new staff started. They didn't know what it would be, but Brendon always had something planned to welcome a new staff member. Like the time a young woman started part-time. The older behaviour specialists tried to warn her. They told her he would test her. They said, here's what he'll do and here's how to get through it. But she didn't believe it, really. I've worked at other places, she told them, I've got this. The first shift she worked with Brendon, she arrived in white shorts and a white t-shirt. It was a morning shift and she would be helping him get dressed. She laid out his clothes and shut the door. And when she opened the door, he threw a big piece of poo at her. I can hear Brendon's excited giggle as he watched her reaction, even through all this time and over all the distance that was and is between us.

Must have been girls in that school too, but I don't remember them. Do you remember, little sister? I see only the boys when I enter that school through the corridor of memory, and the boys I see are uniformly pale with tender eyes and thick, gorgeous dark hair, and they are so, so vulnerable. Brendon was different then. A shank of shocking blonde hair—he and I are the two blondes in the family—and an uncanny ability to watch and to wait for the moment when he could catch you off guard.

See, you're laughing now. He'd wait for the right moment then who knows what he'd try to get away with, all the while offering a provocative grin that disarmed anger—well, for most people. Remember the way his shoulders were always shaking as he giggled at you? By the time he left, he was too large for the trampoline, the toy room, and even his bed, I think. He'd become a tall, strong young man, stuck in our world at the developmental age of a three-year-old. Of course adults can't be housed with children. It was a legal requirement that he be transferred to an adult home. But which one? I don't think you heard much about that because what I know I learned by listening to the adults in the hospital in Calgary. There weren't many choices.

There Were Things Going on We Knew Nothing About

VOICEOVER: The ███ Ranch. It sits on the wide-open prairie of Southern Alberta, about a hundred and thirty kilometres south of Calgary. Visits from the outside world aren't encouraged. Even government inspectors have to give advance notice before a visit. But stories do get out. Psychologist ███ ████████████ opened her ranch 11 years ago. The ten clients here can be hard to handle. Tantrums are not uncommon. When that happens, physical restraint is used. The Ranch has a firm policy against excessive force and abuse. But over the years, complaints have surfaced.

Tools you might need if you wanted to build a home along the river, Métis style: broad axe, knife, two-man crosscutter, auger, drawknife, square nails, merits, and wood plane. You'll need to know how to make joints, like the dovetail joint and the joint with a wooden peg.

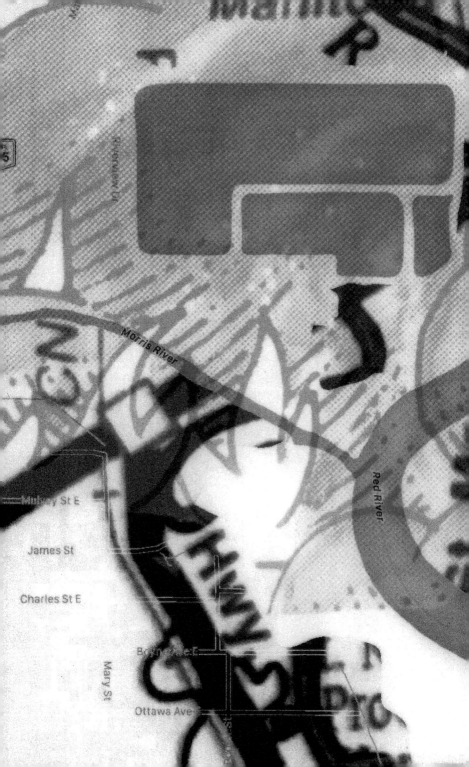

CHAPTER THREE

The Buffalo Hunt at Wood Mountain

The boy's father had a shock of red hair and eyes that didn't match. One eye was green and the other was a colour whose name was always on the tip of your tongue, and yet was every time lost the moment you tried to speak it. There was the boy's sister, younger by five years. And what do they say when they're inviting everyone to sit down between dances and to rest their fiddles or their feet? If trouble didn't turn up for a visit, well, there wouldn't be a story to tell, would there?

Rivers don't want to stay still. I mean most of the time. Sometimes they do pool, and you can be lulled into thinking they have nothing to do with movement, for the moment at least. When a river pools, its movement is pent up and the release you don't see is happening beneath the surface. My brother would be good while he was studying you. He was still until he figured you out, what he could get away with, and what he could do that would annoy you the most. Pools supply movement to the river further down. They pause to build up energy for what's coming next.

I was where I felt most comfortable: on the road again, mama in the seat beside me.

You were at home, I know, and I don't know how that felt. We didn't have a car at the time, I'm pretty sure. In the theatre of my memory, I am sitting in the big soft seat of a long-distance bus with darkened windows.

As a child, Louis Goulet and his family traveled in the direction of the buffalo time after time to Wood Mountain as part of a hunting caravan. The name Wood Mountain comes from the Métis words "Montagne de Bois" It was a name that called to mind the abundance of poplar trees, a notable feature in the Saskatchewan grasslands. Think of the shock of trees on the grasslands, the temporary relief.

North and west of Louis Goulet's Wood Mountain is Wood Buffalo National Park. It's the largest national park in Canada and crosses from the northeastern portion of Alberta into southern portions of Northwest Territories. The park was established in 1922 to protect what was then the world's largest herd of free roaming wood bison. In 2017 stories began appearing in local and national news outlets about the Métis in the area, who said they'd been written out of the history of the land the park was on. These stories tell how the Northwest Territory Métis Nation was asking not only for $120 million in compensation for lost hunting rights, but also for the inclusion of their story in the shared history of the area. Without this story, people were forgetting that Métis hunters and trappers used the park for generations long before the government established the park.

Stories like this travel in unexpected ways. It was too easy for the government to ignore the presence of the Métis and their land rights when they negotiated Indigenous rights to use the land in the park. And back in 2017, if you'd read the official history on the Parks Canada website, it would have told you that all impacted Indigenous people had been granted harvesting rights in the national park even though Métis rights had not been granted. The Métis Nation organized to change this shared history so that today the website includes the story of the Métis struggle to have their rights recognized.

The president of the Northwest Territory Métis Nation, Garry Bailey, said at the time that it was important to tell the true history of what happened to the Métis people when Wood Buffalo National Park was established. People were forced away from their communities, he said. And there's hardly ever any mention about the Métis, he went on. It's as if the Métis never existed there, he said, on the land that is now called the Wood Buffalo National Park. Now, they insist on being seen.

Steep Slopes Fall Against Braided Rivers

Braiding is an action taken against steep riverbanks that erode under the river's pressure. My great-grandfather's crooked tunes are built from notes that erode and let through the braided rhythms of future generations. A traditional Métis fiddler will hardly ever play a song the same way twice. My brother never learned to play fiddle and he didn't know what the word Métis meant, but you never knew what he was going to do next.

Our mama on that ride became a man-made dam, she looked like she was sustaining the incredible pressure of a redirected river, holding back the flow meant to support the life of all the people. You know what I mean because you've seen it too. She still gets like that sometimes. Her pursed lips, her hands gripping one another in her lap. I get like that.

It would have been a Greyhound bus, of course. I can see the long, lean dog on the side of the bus without trouble. We often rode those buses to travel from one community to another when we needed, so I could be transposing the memory of the bus from another journey. I don't think so, though. It'll be remembered like this: on the way to the hospital in Calgary, we coasted down Queen Elizabeth II Highway.

Highway 2. It was a route we almost always had to drive when we were going to Calgary, on our way to the place where mama's firstborn waited, to see our brother, to put our arms around Brendon. The highway was home. Only this time we weren't headed to a home for children. My mother and I were headed to a burn unit in the Foothills Hospital in Calgary.

How to get from St. Albert to Calgary. Head northeast on Sir Winston Churchill Ave North. Turn right onto Green Grove Drive. Turn right onto the St. Albert Trail/AB-2 South. Merge onto AB-216 South.

Take the exit onto AB-2 South toward Calgary/Edmonton International Airport. Drive on Highway 2 for approximately 281 kilometres. Take exit 256 for Memorial Drive West, Calgary. Which way is the river? Cities and towns you will pass on your way: Leduc, Morningside, Lacombe, Red Deer, Penhold, Innisfail, Olds, Airdrie, Balzac, Calgary.

∞

Mom crocheted a warm blue and red blanket for him. Left albums filled with family pictures in his room. He waited for us. My big brother taking mama by the hand, pulling her into his world. Excited giggles rippling out, he couldn't stay still. He brought mama the branches he'd pull from the trees, little gifts. One hand cupping one ear. A big smile. In a sing-song voice: da-da-da, and da-da-da again.

Mama says how everybody had their theories about what was wrong with Brendon after he stopped talking. That might be why she told us different stories about our brother, too. But the basic diagnosis they kept coming back to was schizophrenia. She always said how they knew almost nothing about how that disease impacts children, their brain development and ability to tell fantasy or delusion from reality, that kind of thing. How was my brother supposed to know that the voices in his head weren't real? They were real to him. Anyway, mom said they didn't have much to go on. That they figured that when Brendon would make those noises, when he'd cover his ear and repeat da-da-da da-da-da-da, he was hearing voices. The experts told my mom that he was probably covering his ear and making noises to try to drown out the voices he didn't want to hear anymore. Probably, they said. Maybe. They weren't sure.

The axles hold the weight of the Red River Cart. One axle attached to two wheels beneath a cart pulled by an ox, or sometimes a horse. The ox has the right hooves for the mud of river crossings. The axles hold all the weight, and they are made of wood, of poplar or oak, and they are trimmed and shaped to minimize friction. But there is friction.

The screeching of a Red River cart can be heard for miles. Wood rubbing on wood. The wheels turn on un-lubricated axles. Grease? Dirt and dust would gather in the grease and wear out the hub and axle that quick. Nobody used grease at first. After a time, some Métis started using iron parts here and there. But iron can't be replaced like wood. On a trip from Scratching River to St. Paul a single cart can expect to have five or six axles replaced. See, if you want to build a cart and you're not using iron parts, you can just walk into the bush and have a new one within a week.

The way we found out is mom phoned down to the adult home to see how he was doing. We figured it must be hard for him to make the transition. He'd been nine years at the children's home. He'd been at the adult home, the Ranch, three months now and they never called her. She called them and he was always fine, basically, they said. Until the one-time mom phoned and they told her that they'd had to take him to the hospital. Nothing to worry about, they said. He'd gotten mild burns. Hospital was going to keep him overnight. Okay, mom said, okay.

It wasn't until she hung up that mom got to thinking. You know how moms worry and how things like this just kind of develop a life of their own. She thought, if she's the guardian, why didn't anybody from the hospital call her? They'd have to get permission.

Something didn't sit right about that, mom said.

She picked up the phone and dialed the hospital. I can see her on the worn-out brown couch we had, her fingers trembling already.

She asked for the head nurse and when she got her on the phone she asked, how come nobody contacted her? Well, you're not put down here as the guardian, the nurse said. And it's not minor burns either. It's third degree and he's going to be here a long time. Hold on, the nurse said, I'll get the doctor.

There Were Things Going on We Knew Nothing About

VOICEOVER: In 1985 social services removed 5 clients because of concerns about rough treatment and poor living conditions. Eventually ▮▮▮▮ got them back. But the problems persisted and government documents show the department failed to act. In March of 1990, ▮▮▮▮ is "filthy", clients are "unkempt and dirty" during a government inspection. The recommendation: closure. The action taken, none. In April 1990, social services witnessed physical abuse of two clients during an inspection visit. The recommendation to Minister John Oldring, revoke the license. But nothing was done. In October of the same year, department workers interviewed dozens of former staff and residents. They all tell similar stories of physical and psychological abuse, safety violations and filthy living conditions. The recommendation, don't renew the license. But again, nothing was done. In February of 1992 a briefing note to Minister John Oldring says ▮▮▮▮ residents are still "at significant risk." The recommendation by senior officials. Don't renew the contract, but nothing was done.

What to consider when fixing the wheel of the cart:

- the perpendicular bounce,
- the horizontal swing and tug left and right, and
- how the saucer-shaped wheel absorbs these two motions

To make a life from the Red River carts, you've got to keep them in good condition. That way they'll be able to carry 450 kilograms of goods to trade at St. Paul's and can carry 450 kilograms back to sell up at The Forks. These trips bring a kind of wealth you didn't see before the carts began traveling up and down the trails east and west, north and south, carrying buffalo hides and other goods for sale or trade across North America. With a good strong cart, you'll be able to bring enough hides, meat, and pemmican to last you and your family the year, maybe two, after a hunt at Wood Mountain or Cypress Hills.

Wood Mountain today, a little village of about a dozen houses. Grain elevators still standing. It's remembered now mostly for the North-West Mounted Police detachment that opened in 1874 and closed the following year. But the land remembers the Métis and is certain that the Métis will not forget.

THREE HOMES CLOSED: ASSAULT ALLEGATIONS AT AUTISTIC FACILITIES

Chris Dawson and Ashley Geddes.
Calgary Herald; Calgary, Alta. 29 Jan 1993: A1/ FRONT.

cont'd:
Calgary's Louise Murphy said her son Kevin, 33, has been at the ranch for almost three years and Murphy has nothing but praise for the facility.

"I know that you have to use force and you have to use restraint — I lived with it for 20 years," she said, arguing most people have no idea what it's like to deal with people like that.

▮▮▮▮ has been the target of several past investigations.

We were at the hospital a few days before mom asked the nurses about it. It took mom a while to get up the nerve, but when she did the nurse said, thank God. She went to get one of the other nurses and they answered mom's questions about the workers from ▮▮▮ Ranch. Mom said how we were concerned about how the workers would treat Brendon, that they told her they couldn't say anything unless mom asked them direct questions. They weren't allowed, legally. That's when mom got the Ranch workers banned from coming in. That's when mom took over.

∞

THREE HOMES CLOSED: ASSAULT ALLEGATIONS AT AUTISTIC FACILITIES

Chris Dawson and *Ashley Geddes.*
Calgary Herald; Calgary, Alta. 29 Jan 1993: A1/ FRONT.

cont'd:
"What we saw there, frankly, was a reign of terror: broken bones, broken collar bones and other physical and mental abuse," Martin said.

"But, incredibly, this government did absolutely nothing about this situation while this cruelty raged on," Martin added, calling for Cardinal's resignation.

Red Deer MLA John Oldring, previous social services minister, admitted department officials had previously advised him to shut ▮▮▮ down, but said there wasn't "sufficient evidence" or grounds to remove the licence.

∞

The memory of the plains leans on the back of a buffalo mother. The memory of the plains is stored in the hunt of the people.

∞

Mom had so many questions for the nurses. Like why did he have wounds all over him, little circular burns over his genitals and thighs? Why couldn't Brendon sit up? Why was he unable to feed himself? A couple of the workers from the adult home came forward—not the ones who'd been there when he was burned—who said Brendon should have been in the hospital at least a week before the burns. Because he couldn't move. He'd been unable to sit up. They'd had to carry him physically from one place to another, lift him from laying to sitting in bed. There had been something wrong with him even before the burns. God, we wished Brendon could talk.

Red River Cart

Designed for the wide variety of travel conditions it was sure to encounter, the cart was easy to draw through bogs, was buoyant at river fords, strong on rock-strewn paths and hard to upset in stumpy forests. The body was made of tough, well-seasoned oak.

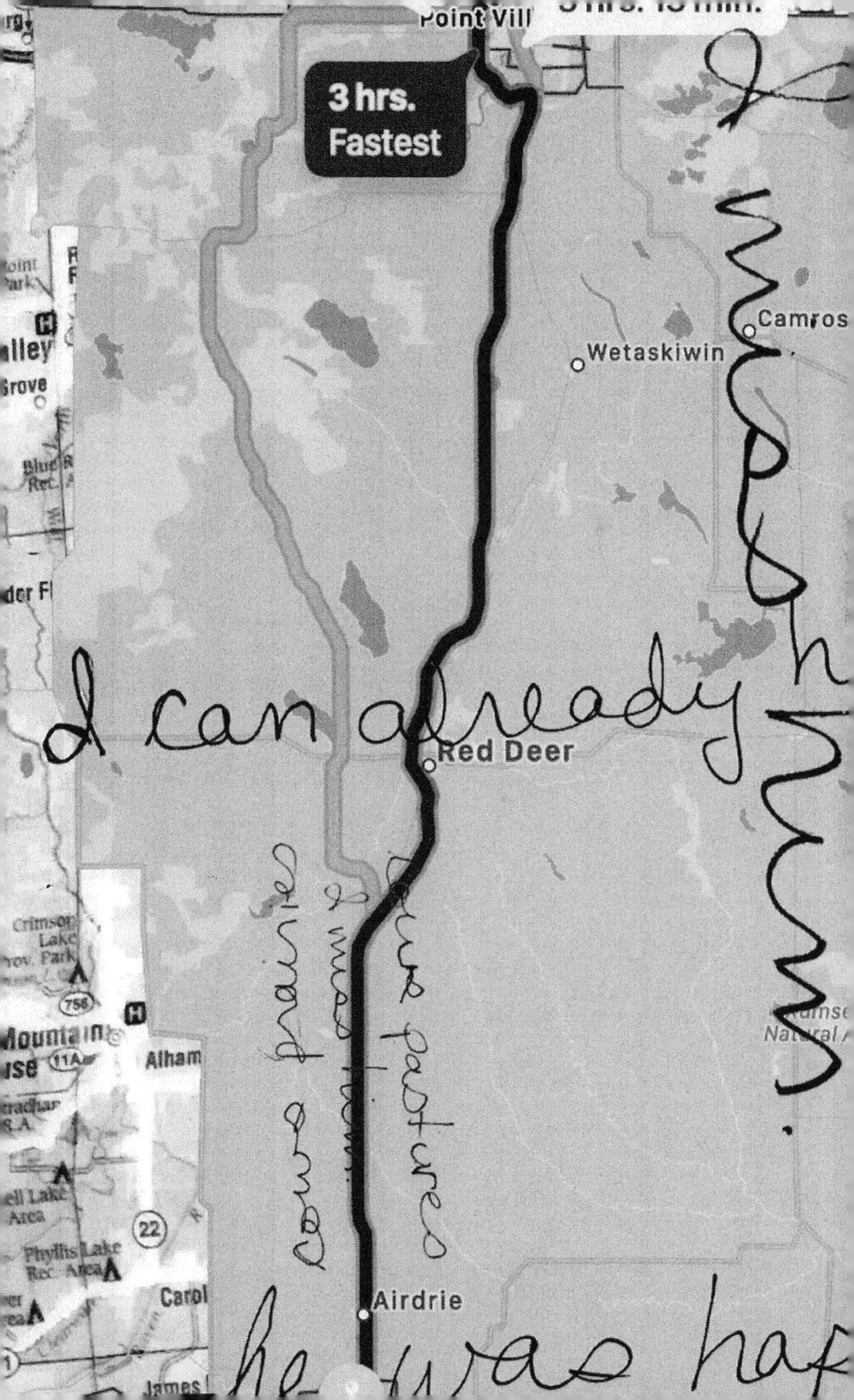
Point Vill
3 hrs.
Fastest
Wetaskiwin
Camros
Red Deer
Airdrie
Alham
Carol
I can already
he was haf

Sturgeon Point Villa

Bridgeland

Options

3 hrs.
318 km · Fastest route

3 hrs. 45 min.
368 km

3 hrs. 13 min.
311 km

ear him giggle.

spy there.

CHAPTER FOUR

When the Buffalo are Scarce: Moving Down the Missouri River

The boy inherited two blessings and one curse from his mother. In no particular order these were: the insatiable urge to be moving on; the ability not to be found; and the near-invisible sash that was around his waist when he came from his mama's body, finger-woven in stripes of different colours with black borders for the hard times.

Did you ever go back to see the children's home he lived in? After he left it, after we'd all grown up, I mean? I did too, once. It wasn't an intended visit. I hadn't meant to go there.

When Rivers Scour Your Landscape

Rivers alter the landscape as they travel through. They say my great grandfather could upend a room by playing a tune. My grandmother was a looker, and when she was performing she could take hold of a hostile audience, turn it any way she wanted. Her sister spoke to you with her fiddle and undid the person you thought you were going to be. If you were to meet my mama, you'd never forget for one moment that you were on her stage. And as for my brother, I've heard people speak of him with a tremor in their throats because his unexpected laughter opened channels in their lives. Change can take time, but in the end rivers scour, they dissolve, and they abrade.

Four main groups of buffalo and how to recognize them, if you lived in 1860s or thereabouts (according to Louis Goulet):

- The Missouri Buffalo have a bristly earth-brown coat, a slow and heavy gait, are terrifying when wounded, no fun to meet up with, and are rarely seen outside of Southern Missouri.
- Prairie Bison live north of Missouri, include the Red River Bison, are shorter in body so sturdier and faster on their feet, and were the primary source of food for Métis for three quarters of a century.
- Saskatchewan Herd/Beaver River Buffalo are called Beaver River Buffalo after a tributary that flows into the Assiniboine, are easily recognized because they are smaller than the others, lasted longer than the Prairie group—some were still there in 1885.
- Wood Buffalo are darker—even black; are the heaviest, stayed in the woods along the Saskatchewan River and around the lakes in Winnipeg, winter in the south— Louis recalls killing some next to the border between Texas and Mexico; and are harder to hunt because they will scatter and plunge into the bush.

All together, these herds extended west from the Mississippi River and the Great Lakes of Ontario to the shelf of the Rocky Mountains, and south from the Gulf of Mexico to the Great Slave Lake on the fringes of the Arctic Circle.

Do you remember that I went with mom? She packed a bag and caught a bus to take us the 318 kilometres from St. Albert to Calgary, and there I was waiting for the bus, all my fourteen years standing next to her bag, scared and silent and branching over her.

And you're right, I think our big sister was the one to babysit you and our little brother. You remember watching a lot of television. You remember that old bunkbed, the one we shared. Sitting on the bottom bunk, left behind. You were twelve, I suppose. The newspaper articles I've read said this all started in February of 1990. I'll have to trust the newspaper articles and journalists: I remember neither dates nor the passing of seasons.

∞

There are just four things bison need: food, water,
other bison and room to roam.

—Eric Rosenquist, The Nature Conservancy

∞

Back then, pediatricians and psychiatrists used to think autism was really rare. Maybe three to four kids per 10,000. Now we know it's closer to one in 68. Back then, Brendon was never diagnosed with autism, but today many of his behaviours would fit into what we now call the autism spectrum.

Our brother's life, it kept moving on while we were away, kept finding the easiest way between here and there. Our brother's life went underground sometimes, or so it seemed to us.

The people who worked with him said that one of the things that makes Brendon unique is that he's more socially interested than a child with autism was ever expected to be. A lot of the kids in that childhood school with Brendon lived entirely in their own world and didn't notice people. If you walked in the room, they probably wouldn't look up. But Brendon, he was always interested in people and in figuring out what made people tick. He was interested in causing a ruckus and getting a reaction. He'd do something he knew he wasn't supposed to do and then he'd look over at whoever he was with and do that hud-dah noise, like do you see what I just did? He still does that, sometimes.

∞

I was walking somewhere else in the neighbourhood, having forgotten his old school was in the area, and I turned the corner and there it was. I'd turned back in time and stepped into the future at once. It made me float a little. It made me think all I had to do was walk to that door again and ring the buzzer and my big brother would be there, still wearing his child's skinny body, hardly able to contain his excitement at seeing me, with one of his teachers nearby to tell him not to do this and not to do that. For his own good. All I'd have to do was say come with me and he'd hold my hand and we'd walk out of that school for good.

But he wasn't there that day and so I walked on.

When we left Calgary, he stayed behind, in that home for children with autism, so he tied us to Calgary. He was nine when he went there to live, when my mom made herself turn her back on him and walk to the car where her mother waited to drive her back to their rental unit, to a red-headed husband, to the three younger daughters already born and tumbling over each other in nightgowns and undershirts, and to the future where another son would be born.

Walking by his old childhood home, I recalled how we never really left Calgary while he was a boy. It was only when he became a man that we all left, after looking for a home for him, after trying one place after another that didn't work, after finding the group home he lives in now, in Edmonton.

Edmonton is our compromise between what we wanted for him and what resources there were for adults like him, the ones with mental disabilities and irreverent spirits. Calgary will always be his childhood. Edmonton is something else. In Edmonton he encountered the man that he is.

What you may have seen on Carlton Trail / Piste Carlton between the 1860s and 1880s:

- Métis families moving west, disillusioned with the political developments in Manitoba and
- incoming settlers from eastern Canada hoping to homestead.

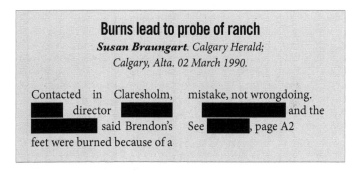

Burns lead to probe of ranch

Susan Braungart. Calgary Herald; Calgary, Alta. 02 March 1990.

Contacted in Claresholm, ▇▇▇ director ▇▇▇▇ ▇▇▇▇ said Brendon's feet were burned because of a mistake, not wrongdoing. ▇▇▇▇ and the See ▇▇▇, page A2

My big brother pulling us all into his world. One hand cupping one ear. An impish smile. In a sing-song voice: da-da-da, and da-da-da again. Da-da-da. We went, all of us.

My little sister doesn't remember that first phone call, when we found out he was in the hospital. She recalls how upset she was after we all got home. Because nothing really happened. It's like the boogeyman, she always says, because there was no face to who did it. Nobody was arrested. She uses the word justice. There was never any justice, she says when she talks about it.

Prairie Ecology and Buffalo

- Strong family bonds helped bison survive.
- Wads of buffalo hair become nest material for other wildlife.
- Buffalo wool was once collected to keep babies warm.
- Buffalo provide for others.

> *I believe that the most important thing for us*
> *as Michif people is land. If we have land, then we*
> *have a place to nurture our future generations....*
> *I think it says a lot about our people that we*
> *still have a strong sense of culture and that our*
> *language is alive. I have never been in a Michif*
> *community where the culture is dying. Ever.*
>
> —Maria Campbell's words on a plaque
> in a museum in Winnipeg

Mom says the problem with getting an accurate diagnosis was that he showed signs of a little bit of everything. Now they have him down as schizophrenic and autistic. She says that for a while back then, they didn't have any idea what was wrong.

Once, mom told us about the advice our family doctor gave her. He said, Just put him in an institution and forget you ever had him. He said, He'll bring you nothing but heartache.

There Were Things Going on We Knew Nothing About

REPORTER: Are you Trevor Hoffman?

HOFFMAN: Sometimes.

VOICEOVER: The latest controversy involves Trevor Hoffman, a ███ worker who recently pled guilty to assaulting this resident, Michael Elder. The way Hoffman tells the story, the whole incident was not much more than a bothersome court appearance and paperwork.

HOFFMAN: No, I pled guilty to physically assaulting him. Just to get the process through and finished and done and that was it.

VOICEOVER: Hoffman didn't want to talk about the case. But in the court transcript, the crown prosecutor gave the details. Hoffman lost control and kicked Mr. Elder in the face, and while Mr. Elder was down on the ground, the accused pulled Mr. Elder's hair and put it into Elder's mouth to humiliate Mr. Elder. Trevor Hoffman pled guilty to this. He was fined $300.

REPORTER: What justification can there be for physically punishing an autistic young adult?

HOFFMAN: For physically punishing a young adult? It's not justifiable. Not.

He was mama's first-born child. She said he seemed perfectly normal to her until she brought our older sister home, her second born child and her first daughter. Brendon would have been about seventeen months then. That's when he started losing everything, mama said so many times. He'd seemed like a normal kid. You'd say nose and he'd touch his nose, and then his eyes and his ears. All of it. She brought her second child home and he just stopped doing all those things. It wasn't that he didn't have the intelligence, she said. That was what baffled her about it all, and frightened her. It was just that he didn't want to do most of it anymore. And later, after he left home, he'd be able to figure out how to get out of locked hospital wards and escape from institutions. Mom always said how smart Brendon was and is, but it's for what he wants. He didn't want to point to noses and ears anymore, he didn't want to learn letters, he didn't want to sleep through the night anymore, he didn't want to stay in the house—he refused it all.

These were the days before seat belts. We slept leaning over each other, like puppies, lying head in the lap and ear to spine. When we were driving late, in the rush of headlights against the night, I'd crawl up to the back dash to sleep, huddled in the little space against the rear windshield. They'd wake us when we got there.

We came together around the channel bars, the bits of land that showed through the course of our braiding rivers.

During the day it was always bright, no matter the season. I don't recall any rain while we were driving to Brendon's. Do you? Nor any snow—not falling snow. The light was the kind that ran across a big sky and back just because it could; and because it loved the cramp of muscle in its legs after a sprint and the thrilling bang boom of the heart in its chest; and because the light needed to be tired at the end of the day so it could sleep large and still and deep as the prairie night.

CHAPTER FIVE

At the Speed of an Ox: The Hunt in Cypress Hills

From the boy's father arrived two curses and one blessing. In no particular order, these were: thick white hair, the ability to see into more than one world, and a diagnosis of childhood schizophrenia. Where the autism came from, no one knew.

Organize a Hunt. Spread the word through the church and word of mouth. Be ready with your cart and your family when the caravan passes.

Bring the assembly together for the election. Elect the leaders of the hunt. First and second leader and the Council of Twelve.

The Council decides the laws of the hunt. Order is necessary to protect against attack and to prevent reckless behaviour. Young people can get carried away. Without discipline, they'll ride into the middle of a herd, foolishly. Or they'll let loose a stray bullet and end up squaring off with a bull, wild with fear and pain.

Intergenerational Trauma Regularly Fluctuates

Braided channels tend to form in rivers with a large sedimentary load and where discharge regularly fluctuates. It took decades for me to understand the geomorphology of our family history, that we were each of us carrying loads shaped by the irregular discharge of intergenerational trauma. Our brother's life went underground sometimes, or it seemed that way to us. Our brother's life flooded into ours sometimes too, and we waited by the floodplains with him for the waters to recede.

Spanning the southeast corner of Alberta and the southwest corner of Saskatchewan is the Cypress Hills Interprovincial Park. If you're in Alberta and you want to get to the park, get yourself on Highway 41, in some places it's called Buffalo Trail. The park is a one-hour drive from Medicine Hat. The speed limit along most sections of the trail is 100 kilometres per hour. There's a heritage park on the south side of the park in Alberta, called Fort Walsh.

The story goes that they built Fort Walsh in Cypress Hills for Northwest Mounted Police Superintendent James Walsh in 1875, whose mandate was to curb whiskey trade and to police/harass the Sioux living there. This was only two years after the Cypress Hills Massacre. Métis families had occupied and re-occupied a winter village site along the northwest slope of Cypress Hills before, during, and after this time. Today, tourists tour the reconstructed fort, the former townsite, the cemeteries, and the whiskey trading post.

The history of the place goes on. In 1877 Assiniboine Chiefs Man Who Takes the Coat, Long Lodge, and Lean Man signed Treaty 4 with the British Crown. That was on September 25.

James Walsh was there. And in that same year Chief Joseph and his people, the Nez Perce, were on the way to Cypress Hills, hoping to seek refuge on the land from the American army, but they were captured near the Bear Paw Mountains before they could get there.

More treaties were signed in the years after. A rebellion was quashed. A resistance starved into submission and then more treaties. The people belonging to the land had to move on to make room for a life without the buffalo and without the grasslands. People moving on and on. Settlers brought farming and ranching, and this in turn changed the landscape so that by the turn of the twentieth century, cattle was the dominant grazing animal, replacing those productive buffalo migrations. Cereal grains replaced the oceans of prairie grass that once fed the buffalo, the soil, the ecosystem, and all the people.

The Métis diaspora, we are a braided river channel, a herd of bison on our way to the grasslands up the way, to our relations. They wanted us to recede, to dry up, to go underground. People wanted the Métis to stop flowing. But we didn't.

Farming and ranching are still a part of the lives of the people living around Cypress Hills. Recently prairie bison were re-introduced to the Grasslands National Park, which is three hours east of the Cypress Hills Park on the Saskatchewan side. Bison had been absent for 120 years.

One of the workers told me she cried and cried the day Brendon turned eighteen, the day he left the children's residence and school, the day she had to say goodbye.

∞

The land Louis Goulet and his family belonged to had changed since they'd last been there. "Every last leaf and head of grain devoured," Louis recalled.

Louis was nine years old that year.

He and his family had been traveling for two years, from St. Norbert to the highlands of the Missouri River.

Grasshoppers had destroyed the crops. "I remember seeing the devastation, the wood and fields stripped bare," he said.

The altered landscape in and around St. Norbert was a shock.

Before reaching St. Norbert, they encountered buffalo at Cypress Hills and Wood Mountain, each herd so enormous it could be called a foule.

On the trail back to St. Norbert they were traveling with a five-hundred-cart caravan.

There Were Things Going on We Knew Nothing About

VOICEOVER: Brendon Porter is a ███ survivor. He's in an Edmonton group home now, but he's got scars to remind him of the Ranch. Brendon received third degree burns to his feet from hot water in a bathtub. To the media, social services said it was an accident. That Brendon was left lying in a tub unattended and used his feet to turn on the hot water. Brendon's mother never bought that for a minute. At the time of the burning Brendon was weak and lethargic because he was being taken off his medication.

BRENDON'S MOM: The burns aren't from sitting in a bathtub. And Brendon couldn't have turned on the taps. Brendon couldn't even sit up. He couldn't move his hands, he couldn't do anything. None of it makes any sense now.

VOICEOVER: Internal documents show the government doesn't believe it makes sense either. They really don't know what happened. But they didn't tell that to Donita Porter.

BRENDON'S MOM: I don't know why I was never given any

information like this. Or told anything different. It's almost I feel like I've been brushed aside.

VOICEOVER: The Porter incident generated a flurry of interest in ▉▉▉ Ranch. The local health officer was called in to check the hygiene.

Select your hunters and soldiers. Select your guides and the scouts who know best how to find herds of buffalo and criers who will pass along what everyone needs to know.

What to Take on a Hunt

Everything you own. One to three horses that will fatten on the prairie grasses and be ready to run buffalo when the time comes. A few oxen to yoke and pull the loads that have to be carried every day. As many carts as you can manage. They can be built new or maybe you've repaired them over the past two winters. Buffalo robes and blankets for the night. Usually you sleep on the ground. Kitchen utensils and necessary dishes. Basin(s), pails made from a keg that'd been sawed in half, guns and ammunition, just enough to hunt small game along the way or to fight off attackers.

The prairie provided the rest, said Louis Goulet in *Vanishing Spaces*: "from the clear cool water of a spring to the wild berries, ever changing according to season and type of soil."

While Louis was a boy, his father went along on hunting expeditions as a trader, not a hunter. Goulet's father would lead between ten and thirty carts.

His father's carts were loaded with goods they could trade for buffalo skins and robes, dried or smoked pemmican meat, rawhide, doeskin, sinews, marrow, and furs.

Goulet's father didn't represent a commercial trading company. He "was in business for himself—what they called an independent."

Traders were welcome everywhere: all tribes "looked favorably on any trader, their presence gave protection to the hunters they followed."

Goulet recalled these grassland journeys with such evocative language that it's hard for the reader not to want to be there: "We would travel at the speed of an ox towards the setting sun through the vast fragrant air of the endless plain, stopping only for meals and to camp at night in tents or under the stars if the weather looked promising for the next day…"

Goulet's father sold tea, sugar, salt, pepper, flour, gun powder, cotton, flannel, chintz, fine and coarse linen, wool blankets, knives, and other utensils.

My big brother, pulling. One hand cupping one ear. That smile of his. In a sing-song voice: da-da-da, and da-da-da again. Da-da-da. Pulling.

Hardly any buffalo in sight after the hunts at Wood Mountain and Cypress Hills.

The buffalo were struggling to cope. They were about to lose almost everything.

Many years later, as a blind old man, Louis recalled how "the disappearance of the buffalo from the Red River Valley in 1868 resulted in nothing less than a complete revolution in the life and economy of our country…. What's more my parents, as hunters of the open plains, could feel changes coming they didn't like and weren't ready to accept on short notice. These were things over my head, of course; I was barely ten years old, too young to realize their importance."

They could all see it was coming: one day the buffalo herds at the centre of their lives would vanish.

This absence would become the centre of their lives for a while.

The Red River carts would continue traveling the trails, but they wouldn't be following the buffalo, they wouldn't be filled with fur and meat and pemmican. They would be paid to transport goods between forts and trading posts and countries. The carts would become the first transport trucks of the Prairies.

Burns lead to probe of ranch
Susan Braungart. *Calgary Herald; Calgary, Alta. 02 March 1990.*

...Porter said her son is marked on his legs, arms and face. "Some of the marks to me look like cigarette burns. They're just a round circle into the flesh with no bruising..."

What Do You Do After The Buffalo Are Killed? (According to Louis Goulet)

Strip the meat and make pemmican. This took about three weeks in the summer of 1867, when Louis was nine and his family was returning from the Missouri River.

Steps

1. Claim your killed animal.
2. Skin it on the spot.
3. Hang the hides on stretchers, a kind of frame made of straight poles. Dry and smoke them in the sun until they are stiff as shingles.

4. "Enlever la maque." Scrape the hides to remove the hair and other fat still stuck to the skin. Scraping hides is men's work. But women step in when they have time.
5. Cut the carcasses into thin strips so they dry quickly. Lay the strips on grids of branches over smoking fires of buffalo chips. The buffalo chips drive away the flies. This is women's work. This will take about two days.
6. Put the dried meat in skin bags or baskets made of wicker, rushes, or leather.

To Make Pemmican:

7. Pound the dry meat with a stick, the head of a hammer, or a small stone. Put this in a cast iron pot full of boiling fat or marrow.
8. Cook into a paste.
9. Add dry or crushed berries.
10. Pour the boiling paste into bags made of peau de batterie sewn up with tendon or rawhide to form an air-tight seal.
11. Leave the bags to dry. They'll get as hard as tallow.
12. The older the pemmican, the better it is.

Don't Know How to Eat Pemmican?

13. Straight from the bag.
14. Roast or boil it in its grease.
15. Boil it in dumplings in a stew.

Who Do You Sell To?

16. Hudson's Bay Company is the main market, who sends it west or north, or to England.
17. The St. Paul trading outlet in the United States.

∞

What would you hear on the hunt? (According to Louis Goulet)

Barking. Hundreds of dogs tagged along with the caravan.

These dogs "made a chorus for the incessant din of wooden hubs thirst for grease squealing all day long, announcing our presence for miles around."

The sounds of night. "Thousands of bulls bellowing, shaking the earth with roars and battle cries." And the prairie dogs yapping, the coyote worrying and calling, the wolves howling.

The birds: "How can I describe the song or the cry flung back and forth between two whippoorwills?"

La Biche River

Saddle Lake

Saskatchewan River

bert

Edmonton

COLD LAKE

Fort Pitt

PRIMROSE

AIR WEAPONS RANGE

Primrose Lake

Provincial Reserve

Marie Lake

Primrose Lake

Red Deer River

Crane Lake

Meadow River

919

55

Cold Lake

Mar

insert prairie m

River
Lac la Biche
Beaver Lake
Cold Lake
Frog Lake
Loon Lake
Turtle
Onion Lake
LAKE
RANGE
River
River
Cold Lake
Pierce Lake
chicken here

CHAPTER SIX

The Birds of the Plains

*But between all his blessings and his curses, by the time he
was three he found he'd forgotten how to use his tongue and
he'd forgotten how to find his way back home when he left.*

You may not know what a lek or a booming ground is, nor
what it has to do with a bird called a prairie chicken. I didn't.
Though I knew I immediately loved both of those words the
moment I encountered them in a magazine article.

Louis missed the low sound of the prairie chickens he
heard dancing on leks or booming grounds when he and his
family camped beside their carts on the trails in the spring
and the fall. The way Louis heard them, in large numbers on
the grasslands the birds need to survive, hasn't been heard in
over one hundred years.

I've never been to a lek. Its geography wasn't a possibility in
my imagination and there were no booming grounds in any
stories my mother told me. But my elder-auntie told me in the
strongest terms that I had to get my hands on a copy of this
book that held Louis Goulet's recollections and memories.
And I found leks there, in his memories.

Prairie chickens gather on leks to dance twice a year, spring and winter. Louis Goulet said how it was taboo to hunt and kill prairie chickens during these dances. "It was supposed to be bad luck. Just superstition you might say, but it was certainly a more effective kind of protection than the conservation laws nowadays," he said in *Vanishing Spaces.*

And he goes on talking about the dances that were part of the old prairie lands: "Before cultivation gobbled up the greater part of our [virgin] lands, the whole countryside used to vibrate with the wild rhythms of that dance [of the prairie chicken]..."

And weren't we in the air above the road that day, the length of the bus our wingspan? And weren't we prairie whippoorwills, flushed out into the open and looking at everything through a window as we traveled?

We flew over the farms and ranches. The waving fields of canola. Off ramps, farms and ranches. Houses and barns on Gasoline Alley. Strip malls and alfalfa, wheat, barley.

We didn't see Stony Plain, Samson, Pigeon Lake, Louis Bull, Siksika, Tsuu T'ina, Stoney, Piikaani, Nakoda. We didn't hear the singing of the treaties, Treaty 6 and Treaty 7, true and clear from 1876 and 1877.

There Were Things Going on We Knew Nothing About

HEALTH OFFICER: Well, we didn't do a count of flies but there were lots of them flying around the common room where we were.

VOICEOVER: But it wasn't the flies inside the Ranch house that alarmed Dr Black.

HEALTH OFFICER: There was one of the young men, one of the clients there who had apparently refused to eat his meal and the attendants they were encouraging him to eat his meal by in effect putting a headlock on him, pulling his hair to get him to open his mouth and then shoving the food in through his mouth with a spoon, a degree of force and coercion that I really felt was inappropriate. (*Tape fades in and out.*) There was another young man who had been asked to put on his boots to go outside who had refused to put them on. So in this case three of the staff wrestled him to the ground and forcibly put his boots on, and the last I saw of him they were dragging him outside and took him off to one of the outbuildings.

REPORTER: You're a doctor but you're also a human being. What was your reaction to what you saw that day?

HEALTH OFFICER: I was angry. I was extremely angry.

VOICEOVER: Angry enough to write social services. The department's response, a thank you note.

Before you can return prairie chickens to the land, you'll need to restore the ecosystem.

That's what Dunn Ranch in northern Missouri did.

They restored the tallgrass ecosystem on one thousand acres of land that had never been plowed. Today, Dunn Ranch Prairie has 3,300 acres restored to a fully functioning ecosystem.

Once the ecosystem was in place, they were able to re-introduce prairie chickens.

Prairie chickens need plant diversity. They need open spaces for their booming grounds. They need a nesting habitat that isn't too tall with areas of clumpy grass.

And prairie chickens need fire and bison.

Fire clears vegetation and keeps taller plants and trees from establishing on the land, something prairie chickens dislike. Cedar trees will take over if the land isn't burned.

Bison graze heavily on the same open spaces that prairie chickens use as booming grounds. After the rain, bison wallows dry more quickly than the surrounding grassland and this provides a place for chicks who need to dry out and warm up.

The introduction a new kind of plow is related to the decline of the prairie chicken. The moldboard plow intensified the conversion of grassland to agricultural uses as it was introduced to North America in the 1800s. It improved the productivity of farms, but the prairie chicken all but vanished in the wild.

You've got to get up early in the morning to see prairie chickens on their booming grounds. You'll drive there in the dark hours of the morning. It'll be hard to see the birds at first if you're there good and early and it's still dark. Then light leaks over the Prairies and you see the vibrant orange eyebrows of the male and the air sacs in their throats, like two oranges. These are the sacs that make the booming noise.

The male pumps his feet and raises the feathers at the side of his neck until a female chooses him. You can still hear this sound today, if you want to. It's there. People who go there early in the morning sometimes compare the sound of a booming prairie chicken to a low note played on a wooden flute echoing over the grass and sky. It's that sound that Louis Goulet heard all night long. These birds give everything else up when they're mating.

We'd stay in hotels, sharing one room and two beds. Eat cereal with plastic spoons from mini boxes. Couldn't wait to get to the school. Couldn't wait to see my big brother. One hand cupping one ear. In a sing-song voice: da-da-da-da.

Strategic areas for grassland conservation in Southeastern Alberta, according to The Nature Conservancy of Canada

(NCC): The Milk River Ridge, Milk River Basin, Pakowki Lake, and Cypress Uplands natural areas. These feature some of the largest intact tracts of native grass in the province.

The River Carries It All

A fast-moving river does not filter the water because it wants to carry everything along. Mama was always planning the next move, always pouring everything into the future she was going to create, piling everything and us into the back of a truck. The river isn't interested in letting nutrients and sediment settle to the bottom.

AUTISM: GOVERNMENT TOLD OF ABUSE AT PRIVATE TREATMENT CENTRE

Ashley Geddes, Herald Edmonton Bureau and Chris Dawson. Calgary Herald; Calgary, Alta. 03 Feb 1993: A3.

EDMONTON - New documents detailing abuse and other improprieties at the ▮ ▮ Ranch homes for autistic adults have cast further doubt on government claims it had insufficient evidence earlier to revoke the facilities' licenses.

....The documents cited allegations of physical and mental abuse of residents dating back to 1990 and they continued to raise questions why the government failed to revoke the licenses.

Mom was four or five months pregnant with my little brother, mom's fifth and last child, when Brendon had to leave home for the first time. Mom's mom, my grandmother, had a lot to do with it. It was a forced thing. He was nine. They'd been looking at their options, but the institution was refusing to take him, claiming they didn't have the resources to care for a child like him. He'd been going to a day school for children who were mentally retarded—the word retarded was a part of the school's official name then. There he received the only treatment available to a child like him. The trouble was getting him there.

A handicap bus came every morning five mornings a week to drive him and a handful of other children to school. That would have been okay, but Brendon being Brendon, always figured out how to get out of his seat. They couldn't secure him. Grandma's new husband at the time would get on the bus with Brendon and try all sorts of security straps and belts. Didn't matter what it was, the bus driver said she wouldn't even get to the end of the block and Brendon would be out and causing a ruckus.

That last day, the bus driver said if Brendon got out one more time, she had to refuse to take him. For safety reasons, she just couldn't have him loose in the bus. So, on that last morning Brendon went to the day school, grandma's husband got on the bus with a chain and padlock. He chained Brendon with a padlock and handed the key to the driver. And the driver took him all the way to school. Mom always said it shows what the social workers thought of the situation, because she didn't lose all her kids over this.

When Brendon got to the school the teachers and social workers called, saying, This is way out of line. Grandma took that call and I imagine her dark eyes angry and her black hair all done up the way she did every day. She said to those outraged social workers, Look, if you don't take this child you're going to have four other kids on your hands and a woman in a mental institution. The people at Baker Centre didn't want to take him, but they did, on a temporary basis. He couldn't stay for long; they didn't have the resources in place for a boy like him.

The next day, God help her, mom had to pack his clothes.

She'll feel like a bitch over this for the rest of her life. The next morning he's up and awake and happy, and she's his loving mother and there she is packing all his clothes and everything in a bag and he's not coming home and she can't tell him, can't explain anything to him.

Inside a bus driving down the highway you don't hear anything other than the hum of the engine, the people talking or shifting or coughing in their chairs, and the grating sound of your own thoughts. Inside that bus, we didn't miss the sounds of the birds we didn't hear, and moving that fast we couldn't remember who we belonged to.

The prairie spread out under the wheels of the greyhound bus that moved 100 kilometres per hour down the road. From the bus, the prairie I knew arranged itself into strips of concrete and satisfyingly symmetrical fields of crops. Then, I didn't know how to read the history in the land or how to understand the meaning of the little farmyards and the nodding oil pumps that came into view along the side of the road. But I was a poet enough already that I pressed my nose to the glass and asked the land questions it didn't answer, not back then, because I didn't know how to properly ask; did the land, I wanted to know from my soft upholstered seat, think about what it could have been if it had all turned out differently? And on we traveled along the road that had no ending I could see, toward the hospital that held my brother's injuries in a bed with steel railings, white sheets and blue blankets, toward doctors and nurses who offered treatment and medicine and to my brother who would take decades to answer my questions.

What did my dreams consist of then? Just what you could carry with you in a pocket or two, and little more. Anyway, a person could only carry so much. And what could a teenage urban Métis in ill-fitting fifteen-dollar blue jeans, a girl with no proper relations to hold her up, what could she carry with her? Stories. In the end stories turned out to be everything she needed. In the middle and in the beginning, too.

Even before that bus ride, back when he was the beloved child who created this irresistible kind of chaos in everybody's lives, nobody knew how to read my brother's history. They guessed at one thing and then at another. But in those days hardly anyone had any information about what he was or what he could be.

The social workers and doctors couldn't find a place for him partly because they didn't know what he was and partly because there are never enough places for the children who have mental disabilities that are easily named and categorized, never mind a child with my brother's incoherent diagnoses. So before he went to the children's home for autistic children where he lived for nine years, Brendon went to Baker Centre in Calgary.

Baker Centre has had many lives. It was built in 1920 to provide tuberculosis treatment. During the Second World War, Japanese-Canadian detainees were also treated there. In 1962 an addition to the facility was built, the portion that my brother would live in for a time. This was the Baker Centre my mother knew, an extension of the Alberta School Hospital and built for the housing and treatment of mentally disabled children.

They lived alongside each other for nearly two decades, the sanatorium and the treatment facility for mentally disabled children. The sanatorium closed in 1980. During its operation, some say those buildings saw about 10,000 patients, many of whom died within the walls. The Baker Centre began treating and housing mentally disabled adults as well, but not for much longer. In 1989, the buildings were torn down. The area is now a riverside park, across the Bow River from Bowness Park.

But some say the land remembers. Unusual experiences have been reported. Some people have said they feel that they've been watched or that they sense a heaviness or a creepiness. Others have reported that their dogs behave strangely during walks in the park, suddenly freezing in place and refusing to move. There's a group of people involved in paranormal investigations on the site where the buildings once stood. Their goal, they say, is to attempt to make contact with any patients whose spirits may still be attached to the site.

Lots of things mama doesn't talk about at all. But Baker she'll talk about. Let's say I'm on the phone with her right now and let's say I ask her about it.

She'll say off the top, without hesitation, Baker was a hellhole. A pause for her to let her dog in her apartment in the seniors' complex. When us kids moved out, she got dogs.

Then, maybe she'll say, It was horrible.

She might leave it at that kind of a condemnation, and most of the time we're satisfied with that, but what if on this occasion someone asks how was it horrible? She'll say that my brother didn't fit in there.

Let's say she's in the house now and she's sat herself down in her kitchen and the dogs have settled onto the sofa. It was the ward he was on, she might continue. It was the second floor, the one for retarded children. And Brendon wasn't retarded. The workers absolutely hated him because he was so different than the retarded kids. Those kids would basically sit there and be happy. Not Brendon. She might laugh a bit here, lost in memories of the things Brendon could get up to.

She might offer a list of things he'd do and, if she did, she'd start with the doors that couldn't keep him in. The door to get on the ward was split in two and it had two different handles. To get in there you had to turn each door handle a different way. They were high up and you couldn't even reach it, really. So Brendon, what he would do is he'd take some of their equipment or some of the toys and he would jam it against the handles so that he could get out. He could always figure it out and he would take off. He would set off the fire alarms as he was running down the hall. Another time, it was a miracle, there was a delivery man who was coming into the building as the workers were looking for him all over and they said have you seen a boy? And the delivery man pointed to the Bow River. And they had to jump in and get him. The little bugger, mama will say almost for certain. She'll say it with more love than she says almost anything else, too.

If you give her space and time and a bit of silence, she'll tell you about one of her encounters with one of the workers. One of the times, mama might say, I was there to pick him up and along came this worker from his ward and she said, Oh, so you're Brendon's mother." Yes, mom says and the woman explained she worked with Brendon there. And then this woman said, He's Satan himself, your son, he's from the devil.

Mama might laugh then and say that nothing came out of her mouth at first. And she might tell you how she asked the woman, Are you serious? and the woman was. Mama might shake her head while holding her phone to her ear as she tells this story. She might add, These were the workers looking after these kids.

She might then begin talking for a bit about his current workers in the Edmonton adult group home and this will make her feel better. She might talk about this man who works really well with Brendon, the one he likes to spend time with. She might say how Brendon's having trouble working with one of the new female workers who can't get him to do what she wants, but that she's been told it's getting better and the woman is working on it. The man though, he doesn't like to increase my brother's meds, because then he just sits and drools. He likes it when Brendon is up and active.

But she'll talk more about Baker if asked, because the time Brendon was there is in her memory like the day of each of our births. So she might recall how the Baker Centre couldn't handle Brendon anymore. She might take a moment to say that almost no place could handle Brendon. Not the centre for mentally disabled children—or for retarded children as they were called most often back then. Not the home for delinquent boys.

Oh, yes, she might laugh when asked, Oh yes, they tried a delinquent home because they were sure it was bad parenting that made him the way he was. But he could get out of the delinquent home pretty much whenever he wanted, she'll say, and then she might add again, little bugger. Margaret House, the home for autistic children took him because it was the only place that could contain him, with their locked rooms and security. After the burns, after the hospitalization and his recovery at his old home, he went to Michener Centre while they were trying to set up a group home. There it was about fifty clients to four or five nurses. That was horrible, she might say. And then she might add a few of the details she wants to forget: When you walked in there, mom will say, there were people sitting around naked with feces all over them and there were people with serious mental issues. Even Brendon was scared, she'll say, and then add, I didn't know what to do. He was pulling at me and clinging to me. He was trembling and I had to leave him.

She might recall a better Michener Centre too, if given a moment. She'll tell about the last time she saw Michener Centre in Red Deer, Alberta, when she was looking at it again as a place of last resort for Brendon. She might forget to say that that was after he'd been evicted from a group home because one of the care workers quit, a man who said working with Brendon had given him a mental breakdown, and because the other workers also threatened to quit unless Brendon left. Her stories are dense with unfiltered silt. She might forget to say she didn't have much choice. At that point, Michener was amidst a change, she'll say. They were shifting to a program of about eight clients to each ward. It was going to be much better. But I don't know what they did with all those other people, she'll add, because she always thinks about those other people. I really don't know, she'll say, and the sediment she carries from the stories of all these people might make her sigh.

And yet for nine years, the home for autistic children in Calgary, Margaret House, was his to grow in. She won't say that though, and she wouldn't put it that way. She might turn to another story, a story about one of his visits home from Margaret House. Let's say she talks about a visit over Christmas. She might begin with a description of an apartment torn to pieces by her oldest son. And then she'll take you to the hardest part, the four-hour return trip to Calgary. She might not be with you anymore because she's traveled back to the past where her mother is driving the car and Brendon is lunging for his grandmother's neck and arms. Because that's the one thing he really isn't supposed to do. My mother's brother, my uncle, is there in the backseat with my mom and together they are physically restraining her ten-year-old boy and together they can barely do it. This goes against her instinct, you'll hear that in her voice; she wants to be taking her boy to the open land, to take him on prairie trails where he can roam as he likes and she can follow him where he leads. But she can't, and so she'll abruptly take the story from the car and the physical struggle to the walk back up the concrete sidewalk to the front door of Margaret House. Her mom and her brother wait in the car. And she'll tell how she watched him relax as he walked into the school, how he became calmer than he was before. She'll walk out of the door in her story and then turn around, to see him one more time. On the phone in the seniors' complex, her dogs napping, she might say, There he was, at the end of the hall looking out of the great big window there. He was staring out at her. And if she could put words into the way he was looking at her, it was like he was thinking, Thank God, I'm back where I belong.

treatment of mentally disabled children. I
sabled adults

Bak

Opened   1920

Closed   1981

Demolished   1989

Bow River

can't
picture this m
hel

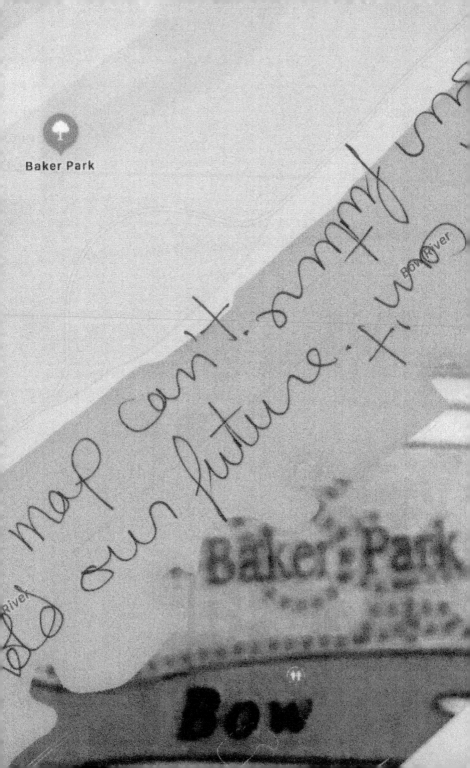

CHAPTER SEVEN

Wintering Over

One day when he was nine, his mother gave him a magic bicycle, a pair of shorts, and a loaf of bread.

Dams Are Linked to Unpredictable Behaviours

A dam interrupts the flow and changes how the energy is released. Pent up, it can be hard to handle. You'll see unpredictable behaviours, including but not limited to erosion, flooding, hitting, spreading excrement on walls, destabilization of the bedding plains, mudslides and attempts to escape.

Winter hunting fills the pot. Bad weather makes for good hunting. Hunt in a blizzard if you can. The animals lay down facing the wind. Their heads are low. The bulls form a half circle at the edge of the herd.

Bulls make good eating in the winter. During rutting season they're awful. Cows? Good all year. But in the lead to spring calving season when the cows are pregnant, we don't hunt them. We let them give us the next generation of buffalo. But if you do hunt a bull out of the winter season, you can get rid of the foul taste by letting the meat dry in the sun or smoking it.

Leave early in the morning, at first dawn. I don't need to tell you to approach from downwind in any season.

When we hunt in the winter, it's to top up the meat supply. Pemmican generally isn't made from winter kill, so it's not as labour-intensive to prepare the meat. Pemmican asks for the sun and the heat.

Burns lead to probe of ranch

Susan Braungart. Calgary Herald;
Calgary, Alta. 02 March 1990.

Brendon recently had skin grafts performed on his feet and is expected to be in hospital for several more weeks. Porter, who lives in St. Albert...

You wanted to be right where I was didn't you? Right there, with mom, with Brendon, in the middle of it. Not left behind. But I think of the girl that I was then. I grope for the words to say to myself, never mind you, what it was for me as a kid to see our brother the way Brendon was. Our irrepressible brother, the family rebel, who no longer used his hands, no longer sat up. No more of that giggling. No more ah-da, ah-da.

No more testing any limits. He lay almost entirely unmoving.

The wounds. You saw them in pictures, later. They were all over his body. Perfectly circular marks or burns that mom and a worker from his childhood school said looked like cigarette burns. They weren't from splashes of water, not those. To the eyes of the fourteen-year-old girl then, our brother looked like he'd been used as an ashtray. He looked like he'd been battered. I look at the pictures you've kept all these years, and there it is, the marks showing outside his blue hospital gown, mom by his side. I don't think there's a picture of me in the hospital, is there? Not a picture of me in Calgary, with mom or with Brendon. It's as if I wasn't there at all.

> *Without being exactly aware of what changes had occurred in the last four or five years, my father knew something was missing in the Red River Colony: there wasn't the same feeling of unity and friendship that had always been felt among people of different races and religions. And he wasn't the only one unhappy about the way things were going.*
>
> —Louis Goulet, *Vanishing Spaces*

The Disappearance of a River

A river gone missing, a rare geomorphological phenomenon that they say will be more and more common as a result of climate change. The disappearance of a river is also linked to trauma. Growing up, my mother never heard the term complex post-traumatic stress disorder. A man who'd reported from war zones told me that he had been trained how to prepare his mind for what was coming. For this reason, he said, he doesn't have PTSD. Only one flashback haunts him—and that, he said, is because what he saw happen in front of him occurred before he'd had time to prepare his mind. Climate change will be like that, unexpected ecological traumas coming on the heels of unpredicted impacts, until the rivers of our intended futures are captured by other currents, until river piracy takes us where we never meant to go.

The burns. You were horrified by the pictures mom brought back? Those wounds that were raw and weeping, that were from another world, not ours. Both feet and one leg. The burns then and the melted skin and scars today rise evenly to just below his knee. The same level all around the leg.

At times of high discharge, braided streams carry a large load of coarse material. This material can become too high for some of the smaller streams at the edge, the ones that have strayed furthest from the deepest part of the main stream. Sometimes the flow will slow to a trickle around the material that has been deposited.

To my eyes the burns told a different story than the one told by the workers, how they left him in a bathtub and Brendon turned on the hot water tap on his own, with his feet. We've talked about this, haven't we? Or did we just talk to each other in our heads?

Case Study

Does the right to hunt extend to the responsibility to protect the bison that is the traditional food source?

The right to hunt that is protected under Treaty 8—signed with the Mikisew Cree First Nations (MCFN) in 1899—includes the traditional winter hunting of the nearby wood buffalo (sakâw mostos). This herd is sometimes called the Ronald Lake herd but, like all bison, has a range that extends much farther, west of the Athabasca River and east of the Birch Lakes in northern Alberta. This herd is shifting its migration routes out of traditional lands. According to a 2015 report by Candler, Leech, Whittaker and The Firelight Group, "while wood bison are now rare and hard to find within MCFN lands, MCFN members maintain a rich set of social, cultural, and knowledge-based practices that rely largely on the presence of a single remaining wood bison herd within preferred and historically known hunting areas."

Increased industrial development in nearby areas threatens to extinguish the ability of MCFN to engage in the traditional winter hunting by disturbing the herd enough that it shifts its migration routes elsewhere. Another herd of buffalo, the paskwâw mostos or plains bison, was introduced to nearby Wood Buffalo National Park in the 1920s. However, this plains bison herd is not the species traditionally hunted by MCFN; this herd is not as healthy as the traditional wood bison herd, and in this case park regulations prohibit the hunting of bison on park land, including hunting by First Nations. There is a very real threat that the MCFN in the area will have the right to hunt, but will no longer have any animals that are healthy or legal to hunt. "The knowledge documented through this study suggests that immediate protection of this herd and its associated habitat may be the only option for protecting MCFN rights to harvest wood bison and to transmit important aspects of Mikisew knowledge, practice, culture, and way of life that are place and bison-specific to future generations," the reports says.

Question:

Does the protection of the First Nations right to hunt extend to the protection of the animal itself, the bison that is the traditional food source?

What's at stake:

The wood bison herd. If the healthy wood bison herd responds to the industrial activity on their land by moving their range into the Wood Buffalo National Park land, they will be exposed to the bovine diseases that are much more prevalent among the plains bison herd there. Additionally, the park's habitat is not as suitable for wood bison, where they will find lower-quality grazing for their needs. If the herd remains in its current range (unlikely), the herd will be exposed to unknown levels of industrial contaminants, becoming less healthy and unsafe to eat. Is this an acceptable impact of new/proposed industrial activity?

The free practice of hunting rights. If the wood buffalo herd moves into the park land in response to the industrial disturbance (which is likely), regulations prohibit MCFN members from hunting. If the wood buffalo herd moves to Birch Mountains in response (a possibility), the difficult and limited access to this area, particularly during winter, MCFN members lose the ability to hunt. If the land and then the bison become contaminated with industrial pollutants, the meat becomes unhealthy and hunters will not be able to hunt.

Culture. The relationship between wood bison and the MCFN "has existed since time immemorial." A healthy herd roaming on healthy land is key to maintaining traditional cultural practices related to beliefs about and relationships with bison.

Land. Pollutants, contaminants, noise, increased traffic and the number of new people working and hunting in the area results in a loss of productive habitat and land for the buffalo's roaming needs. The buffalo is part of the land's ecosystem. The land needs the buffalo as much as the buffalo needs the land.

Health. The health of the people relies on hunting bison that are healthy and uncontaminated.

Options:

- Do nothing. Allow unrestricted industrial development in the area, including the mine expansion.
- Allow MCFN members to practice hunting rights within the limits of Wood Buffalo National Park.
- Restrict industrial development in the area to protect the land as the home of the wood bison herd (an endangered species) and to protect MCFN rights to traditional winter hunting of this wood bison herd.

Desired outcome:

Maintain existence of the herd *and* support harvesting rights.

∞

*As soon as the snow melted in the spring, we would
leave our winter camp as we always did and head
for another location, either farther south or farther
north, around Fort Layusse (Edmonton), or St.
Albert and beyond. Finally we'd return to the Red
River, where the buffalo were getting scarce. They
would disappear completely in 1868, after the
devastation that went along with the grasshoppers.*

—Louis Goulet, *Vanishing Spaces*

There Were Things Going on We Knew Nothing About

EX-EMPLOYEE: They have recourse in the law.

VOICEOVER: This couple used to work at the ███ Ranch.
James Rosso knows about violence and abuse. He freely admits
he used excessive force against this ███ client. Rosso regrets
it.

EX-EMPLOYEE: Apparently, I had grabbed him, thrown
him down on the floor and was standing over him shaking
my finger in his face just screaming. I found out later that I'd
broke his collarbone when I threw him down on the floor.

REPORTER: But you weren't the only one who lost it and
there were others who lost it on a regular basis, I understand.

EX-EMPLOYEE: I don't think they lost it at all. I think they
were doing it because they could get away with it.

REPORTER: What do you mean?

EX-EMPLOYEE: When you see someone in a room kicking
someone because they won't make their bed, that's not losing
it—that's trying to force somebody to do something. That's
abusing your power.

VOICEOVER: He sent a letter to social services, detailing
abuse at the Ranch. Senior officials knew of this letter and
other complaints, but they didn't act.

EX-EMPLOYEE: And I mean I broke bones. I broke a bone, and I still had a job. In fact, after I did that, within a month I was given a raise. A hundred-dollar-a-month raise. They've gotten away with who knows what. And they continue to get away with it and will continue to get away with it until somebody decides to do something about it. Whether this helps I don't know.

Requirements for the practice of MCFN right to hunt bison and current conditions, according to Sakâw Mostos (Wood Bison): Mikisew Cree First Nation Indigenous Knowledge Study, 2015.

- Quality: Animals must be perceived to be healthy, with MCFN able to eat them with confidence.
- Quantity: Sufficient to make harvest worthwhile. Full practice of MCFN right would require at least one accessible bison/MCFN member/year within MCFN traditional territory.
- Accessible: Bison need to be available and accessible in known and preferred locations.
- Seasonal availability: Bison must be harvestable and accessible in winter.

RANCH OWNER SUES CBC

Beaty, Bob. *Calgary Herald;*
Calgary, Alta. 27 Jan 1994: B5.

The owner of the controversial ▮▮▮ Ranch shut down by the province after an autistic patient accidentally drowned in a dugout is suing the CBC for $18 million.

...The action against CBC was launched by ▮▮▮ Re-Education Inc. and its owner ▮▮▮ ▮▮▮▮▮▮, ▮▮▮▮▮ lawyer ▮▮▮▮▮ said Wednesday.

No statement of defence has been filed yet.

Sleep. Oh my God. If he got three hours of sleep a night, he was good. Mom always talked about how she could just fall asleep on the floor back then, while she was playing with all of us. He needed more than she could give him, seemed like. When he was angry or frustrated, he'd break everything he could get his hands on, tear apart his room and our rooms, smear his own feces across the walls. The doctors offered drugs to make him sleep. And even then, mama always says he can fight those drugs. When he was at the Alberta Hospital, mom came to visit just after they'd administered some sort of knockout drug. He was in a straight jacket and in a padded room and they said there's no way you can visit because he's going to be unconscious in a few minutes. Mom insisted in her quiet, gentle way, No, no let me see him. So they rolled their eyes at her and opened the door and he just started giggling and giggling when he saw her. Mom always said how nothing knocked him out. He can fight stuff like that. Eventually they took him out of his straight jacket.

Partial list of MCFN members arrested or charged for hunting bison in WBNP according to Sakâw Mostos (Wood Bison): Mikisew Cree First Nation Indigenous Knowledge Study, 2015.

- Pierre and "Dufeld" Gibot (father and son): hunted buffalo in the 1930s or '40s. Fined and went to jail. Removed from WBNP but their rights never came back. Had to move to NWT.
- Several members of the Wandering Spirit family, "Old Man" and the "Spirit boys'": hunted buffalo in 1930s or 40s. Whole family removed from Park. Had to move to Alberta and NWT.
- Larry Marten: hunted buffalo in mid-1970s. Caught with buffalo meat, which was confiscated.
- Archie Antoine and Harvey Gilbot: hunted buffalo in Park; last problem was in the late 1970s. Went to court three times. $300 fine in late 1970s. Got off twice for killing buffalo in WBNP. Threatened with losing work with Parks.

This river will change shape

Morris River

Anderson Creek

Bell Drain

Pounding
Morris River

llway Ave

5th Ave

H66

Finlay

Bell Drain

River

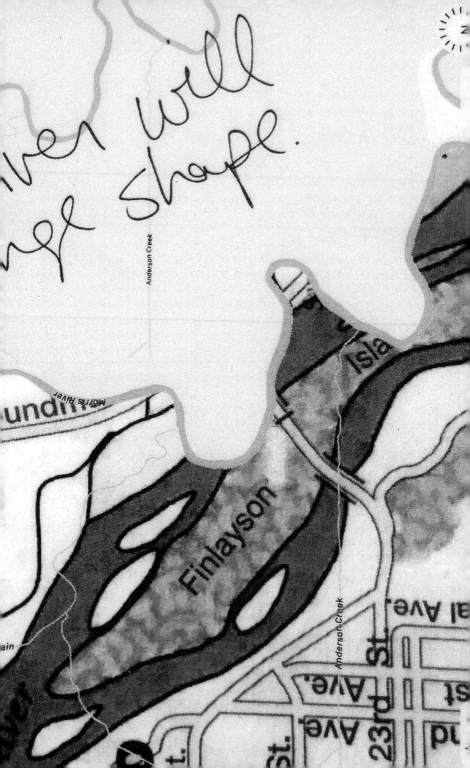

CHAPTER EIGHT

Having a Dance at Judith Basin

Go out to the river at the other end of this world, his mother said. If you cross the river, you'll be healed of all your curses. If you can't find the river or if you can't cross, you'll carry these curses for the rest of your life. He nodded in response because he couldn't talk.

The South Saskatchewan River Basin is a Kokum.

Hardly any other place has as much yearly fluctuation in the water balance as the South Saskatchewan River Basin area. This annual variation is recorded in the rings of trees growing in the Cypress Hills and on the eastern slopes of the Rocky Mountains, holding onto these stories because water is the most important part of growth. The tree rings recall droughts from before the 1880s, the kind of droughts we've hardly seen since. Prairie climates include cycles of drought that have always been unfriendly to settler living patterns—and climate change doesn't promise to make this better. People who study climates and rivers tell us that recent milder drought cycles are not the norm. These mild cycles are aberrations and they are temporary. The normal cycles of severe drought will return to the Prairies again, made worse by climate change.

This last century has been a reprieve. We'll get back to normal, they say.

Tree rings tell stories of the intense drought in the 1790s, when sand dune fields in the South Saskatchewan River became active. They speak of the droughts between the 1850s and 1860s, when the southern Prairies were declared unsuitable for agriculture.

The people who study these things say that there could be higher precipitation in the mountains in winter and spring. The river's dominant flow could then shift from summer to spring. Higher summer temperatures will evaporate more water from river, soil, dugouts, lakes, and reservoirs. The major impact of climate change on the river basin in the long term could be to amplify the large natural variability of the annual water balance. When droughts arrive, they are expected to last longer—decades instead of one to two years— and be more severe.

What we call the South Saskatchewan River Basin begins in the Rocky Mountain glaciers and makes its home in the southern parts of Alberta and Saskatchewan. This system of rivers runs through five major urban centres: Red Deer, Calgary, Lethbridge, Medicine Hat, Swift Current, and Saskatoon. Its relations include Big Stick Lake, Bow River, Oldman River, Red Deer River, Seven Persons Creek, South Saskatchewan River, and the Swift Current Creek sub-basins. The South Saskatchewan River Basin is a kokum, and is part of the Nelson-Hudson Bay Basin, so they're all related and share their stories.

The last time anybody heard Brendon talk. It wasn't mama who heard his last words. The bus driver did. The one who couldn't drive him unless he could be secured in the seat. The bus driver told mama what it was—a complete sentence. Mama doesn't remember anymore what it was. She always sounds a bit sad when she says this. He was six or seven years old then, the last time he talked.

Our brother ran away from all of it. When I saw him in the hospital—when he refused to see, to move, to eat—I thought: He's the strong one. He refused to accept what they did to him, what happened. Some of his workers had said his listlessness and his loss of mobility had started before the burns on his feet. Do you think sometimes that the worst part is not really knowing what happened?

∞

The dance begins:

> *The evening began with a feast.*
> *People outdid themselves to see who could serve the*
> *best meal.*
> *During the feast, there'd be a big singing contest and*
> *after that would come the dancing.*
> *Talk about every kind of reel and jig you could*
> *imagine!*
> *Fiddles, drums, accordions, guitars, Jew's harps,*
> *and mouth organs, anything was fine as long as it*
> *went more or less with the rhythm.*
> *At a shindig like that it was always a contest to see*
> *who could play the best, who could dance the best,*
> *who could sing the best, who could wear through*
> *his moccasins first, who'd be the first to cripple up*
> *with cramps in his legs.*

—Louis Goulet, *Vanishing Spaces*

∞

Parents sing praises of treatment centre program:
[Final Edition]
Susan Braungart. *Calgary Herald;*
Calgary, Alta. 04 Mar 1990: B1.

...Last week, Social Services officials seeking to investigate [Porter's] claims were not allowed to enter ████ Ranch because of a contract between the department and ████████ that forbids unannounced inspections.

My big brother. There he stands at the door looking out at us. One hand cupping one ear. Tapping. Ah-da, ah-da, da-da-da.

The Fires That Come for Your Brother

Some people say the Prairies and rivers could sustain all the people who belong to them again. This requires burning to prepare the land for the buffalo and for the grasses. This means we'll have to survive the fires that come unexpectedly too, the ones that we could have prevented by burning smaller ones, the ones that come for your brother when you think your mother has found a place, a home, finally, for him.

In September 2016, the Autism Society Alberta Board of Directors funded the project "Who Will Take Care Of Our Kids (When We No Longer Can)?" The purpose of this project was to further the Board's understanding of this issue so they can recommend policy changes that will increase access to resources for children and adults with autism, especially quality affordable housing.

He loved his tricycle. Brendon loved that little thing like it was a puppy dog. A lot of times when he would have gone missing, he'd be on his trike. Mom would say how she'd be running around and asking everybody, did you see this little boy? And then, she'd be walking down the back alley and she'd find one of his socks, his shirt, his shorts. Do you remember seeing a little boy? Naked, on his trike? Yeah, they remembered him.

Children begin by finding a tune on the fiddle, a tune that's been there for generations, and then move on by finding that tune in their feet, finding the dance their ancestors placed there, and then pointing their feet in the direction they're going. The Sash Dance was once banned by the Roman Catholic Church. People said that the Church disapproved of the sashes being placed on the floor in the shape of a cross. For the Rabbit-Chase Dance, partners stand opposite each other in male and female lines. The couple at the beginning join and dance down the middle of the two lines, breaking apart at the end and traveling behind their lines until the halfway mark, when the man chases the woman in and out of the lines until he catches her. Then, the next couple dances down the aisle and repeats the performance, but with the woman chasing the man. For the Duck Dance they all trace a figure eight and wind around each other. Then each couple dips under an arch and then stops to make an arch for the others. Outside the circle, by the wall, the older ones are whispering the little ones to sleep. The children, don't they start with a song that's in their milk breath, a song that lives in their fat fingers, curls beneath their hum? A sound that makes them pick up the fiddle and bow and steal away to a corner to try the song waiting in their fingers, to dance what happens next.

There Were Things Going on We Knew Nothing About

VOICEOVER: The ranchers who live around the ███ also have concerns about what's going on there. The people who lived here three years ago found a ███ runaway shivering on the front porch in the middle of the night. Alvin Cornway covered several miles in a prairie snowstorm to get away from ███ Ranch. The reason he ran? He was tired of being hurt.

RUTH ROBB: Anyway, this poor young boy, he was sitting there, and I'm telling him it will be all right all right. He wanted so desperately to get onto a bus and go to his brother. Because he was afraid to go back. He didn't want to go back to this home because he'd been mistreated. And when the RCMP turned up, I guess I felt pretty badly because they walked in with the people from the Ranch and the boy's face just sort of fell down and I thought I'd done something pretty unfair to him. But we didn't have very many choices.

I suppose you and I knew that Brendon returned back to his childhood home, the residence for autistic children, once he got out of hospital. To recover. They invited him back until mom could find a new adult home. And that's where he came back to himself; that's where he recovered; that's where he began to flow again—around the comfort of his regular workers and under their care and love. Did you know? Did I? How could we forget?

Years later, decades later, I called to talk to one of the women who used to work with my brother when she was young. She remembered Brendon right away. She told me things I'd forgotten: How after the burns my brother had returned to that childhood home for autistic children. They all wanted him back, she said. And she said how different he was when he came out of the hospital and returned to the residence. His personality had changed. He just shut down, she recalled. That's part of the reason they agreed to have him back. They thought he should return to something familiar, with people who knew and loved him, to a place that had always been safe.

Prairie grasslands are as ancient as the forests in B.C.

Hardly one of us could say whether we've ever walked near or across unturned, unconverted grassland. The ability to recognize the ecosystem that came before our cities and our highways has been blacked out of almost all our memories. But this memory is planning for the future.

Agriculture reaches deep into the earth and interferes with the soil's ability to heal and to support its own ecosystem. We are part prairie grassland and part river. Did we know this growing up? How could we forget?

A clear-cut is devastating and can take hundreds of years to recover from. But with clearcutting, though you're disturbing the soil, you're not turning the soil, so the forest can recover. A wheat field, however, is not going to find its way back to prairie. There aren't enough pieces left to recover, to reconcile, to understand. That's what they say. And yet, there are prairie reclamations organizations across the continent that are asking the soil to remember what the future is going to look like. Fire, bison, groundhog, prairie.

Woodlands Rd

Westwood Dr

Sir Winston Ch

Boudreau Rd

Wakefield Blvd

Boudreau Rd

Brunswick Cres

Woodlands Water Play Park

Broadview Cres

Fowler Athletic Park

Canadian Tire

Burnham Ave

Beacon Cres

Sturgeon Rd

Sturgeon River

Bernard Dr

Bishop St

St. Albert Centre

BRASIDE

Sturgeon Point Villas

Sturgeon River

Burns St

Birch Dr

Balmoral Dr

DOWNTOWN ST. ALBERT

Brandon St

Muir Dr

Madison Ave

Maple Dr

2

rusted the rive

ee   s there?

We tru

CHAPTER NINE

It's Spring Again and We're Heading to St. Albert

His sister, five years younger. Do you have a bicycle for me? she asked. Their mother shook her head, no. The sister looked around for their father until she remembered he'd been missing for years. So she stood, helpless, watching her brother's back as he cycled away.

There Are Riverbank Histories

My brother was drying up. He had become closed up and so cracked and so oozing we didn't know if he would survive. If it can, a river will keep on moving, no matter what, but there are times when rivers stop flowing. Contributing to the stoppage are factors that include the meander of the river, the history of trauma written in the layers of rocks and sediment, the patterns of autism, schizophrenia, and poverty, and the way these braid themselves across the landscape, and the riverbank histories of the people he doesn't know are his.

$$\infty$$

I don't want to tell you about the water therapy room. I remember it in flashes. The steel butterfly tub. The open room, so much bigger than the room he slept and ate in. The nurses: one at his head and the other at his legs. Maybe more people coming in and out. His legs. His burns. That was it.

Where was he? He'd gone away and what they lifted into the tub was what remained, only burns and pain. Surprising how heavy those two things could be, much heavier than an eighteen-year-old developmentally-delayed boy.

I followed my brother's lead, I followed wherever he went. I waded out into my brother's pain. Then, because it was too much to bear, I went away, too.

This was before they transferred him to Edmonton, nearer the apartment we lived in along the Sturgeon River in St. Albert.

∞

The best thing that happened when we got to the Calgary hospital was when mom finally stood up to the woman who owned ███ Ranch and said she didn't want those workers there anymore. Mom was mad about it all and pretty pissed in her silent way when the woman showed up at the hospital. Mom said the woman tried to talk her out of believing that there was anything wrong and told her that it was all Brendon's fault. Mom wouldn't give in. She said she never saw or spoke to the woman after that. That was hard for her. She talks about what she was like at that time, how she didn't have any confidence back then, how she was scared and timid. After she left our dad, she couldn't make eye contact with people, anxiety attacks, all that. She'll let herself say that it was that hard for her to try and be Brendon's backbone. But then she'll turn the talk to how it would be now, if the same thing were to happen. Now, she'll say, it'd be different. Now, there'd be a fist fight between her and .

When Sediment Settles

Fast rivers carry sand, small stones and sediment that settle on the bottom of the riverbed when the pace of travel slows. My mother didn't want to drop anything, but with five kids and all of us getting heavier and as we grew, she had to slow down sometimes.

In Louis Goulet's time, they had to go all the way down to the Missouri River to find the herds that were central to their way of life. "Finally, later on, when they took refuge in the rough country of Montana, Wyoming, Nebraska and Colorado, it was along the Missouri River we went to find the few remaining herds," Goulet said.

There are no more buffalo hunts near St. Albert, in Cypress Hills, or down the Missouri River. And, for a while a lot of people thought that the way of life led by buffalo was extinct. Now, the stories I'm hearing say there's hope we will find a new path back to the buffalo. Today, the trail that leads back to bison is a kind of moving reconciliation, a painful return to life that requires debridement and the removal of eschar.

I asked mom why she'd taken me with her. She said right away, without having to think, you always seemed to be really close to Brendon. You had a special bond.

My aunt raised her five boys in St. Albert. Her name was Beverly—we called her Aunt Bev—a tall, full-bodied woman who sold Avon and operated a cleaning business. Her house was a safe space. Her hair and makeup were always flawless.

While my brother brought us to Calgary from wherever we were, Aunt Bev brought us from wherever we were to her townhouse in St. Albert.

Aunt Bev was my mother's sister. As a young mother, Aunt Bev followed her mother to Calgary from British Columbia. From there she moved to St. Albert, where she raised her five boys.

Like I said, we were always heading to Aunt Bev's house. Could be we were driving in from another city and staying for a while, sleeping in a line on the thick carpet of her living room floor. Or coming by for the afternoon so she and mom could watch TV or talk over coffee, and we could amuse the youngest boys or take off with the oldest boys to the nearest playground to make up new rules to an old game. Cancer took Aunt Bev some years ago.

All this getting ourselves to Aunt Bev's house in St. Albert happened decades before Thelma Chalifoux founded the Michif Cultural and Métis Resource Institute (now Michif Cultural Connections) in St. Albert. I think Thelma Chalifoux and Aunt Bev could have had a grand talk over coffee and a piece of something sweet. But we never knew Thelma, nor did my Aunt Bev, as far as I know.

The first and only time Aunty Bev's first husband hit her, she took her two sons, and she left. She went to her mom's in Calgary: wasn't going to wait for him to hit her again. It's my cousin who tells me this story, her oldest son. He's proud. He said to me once, "You're more like my mom than I thought."

Aunt Bev believed in rocking crying babies at night, all five of them. Aunt Bev believed in loud music and blaring soap operas. Aunt Bev believed in no rules and letting kids roam. She believed in feeding all the kids who came in her door. She believed in baking perfect, beguiling gingerbread houses that we kids sold door to door. She put a small plaque above her stove that told visitors not to worry about the mess in the house because "it doesn't always look like this/Some days it's even worse."

Aunt Bev rationed milk to make sure everybody got some. Half a cup of milk per bowl of cereal. Aunt Bev believed in getting the family together, bringing them to her house from wherever they got to in the world. Aunt Bev believed in hosting all the weddings in her living room. Aunt Bev believed in having two outdoor barbecue grills in Lion's Park filled with charcoal all day. Aunt Bev taught us how to prepare a tree branch for roasting hot dogs and marshmallows. Aunt Bev believed in sitting with her sisters and having a big laugh and a real good gossip while the kids ran from one side of the huge, treed park and playground to the other—free, untethered, heading back to the safety of the glowing charcoal only when dark got real thick.

AUTISM: GOVERNMENT TOLD OF ABUSE AT PRIVATE TREATMENT CENTRE

*Ashley Geddes, Herald Edmonton Bureau and **Chris Dawson**. Calgary Herald; Calgary, Alta. 03 Feb 1993: A3.*

...An October 1990 memorandum from family and social services regional manager Ilona Boyce details eyewitness reports of residents sleeping in urine, wandering away unsupervised in winter with no shoes or pants, and allegations of physical and mental abuse.

It also said management "ignore incidents of sexual abuse between residents, or sexual abuse of young children" by older residents.

It said "there is no alternative" but to refuse to renew the license at the Claresholm ranch.

∞

Thelma Chalifoux was the first Métis woman to serve in Canada's Senate

Colette Derworiz
SPECIAL TO THE GLOBE AND MAIL
PUBLISHED OCTOBER 6, 2017

Thelma Chalifoux, who fought to reunite her family after losing her children during the Sixties Scoop, and later became the first Métis woman to serve in Canada's Senate, died on Sept. 22 at a critical care centre in St. Albert, Alta. She was 88.

Throughout her life, Ms. Chalifoux was a tireless advocate for social justice and women's rights, particularly for indigenous people.

"We were the Métis and we worked hard," Ms. Chalifoux said in a 2013 video by the Northern Alberta Institute of Technology (NAIT), where she was a Métis elder-in-residence. "I was raised to be strong and independent.

"I would walk into a meeting and they would say, 'Here comes Thelma and her women's lip' and I would say, 'Yes, you better believe it and you better listen to it...'"

The butterfly tub is often used in hydrotherapy rooms. It's the kind of tub Brendon was in every day after he was burned. We couldn't push him in a wheelchair because he couldn't sit up, not then. He had to be wheeled to the hydrotherapy room in a bed. The tub extends its wings to the side to give the nurses lots of room to remove the bandages and to scrape off the dead flesh and infection and clean the site for a skin graft. Debridement or removal of eschar or dead skin is done during daily baths. Eschar must be removed before wound healing or a graft surgery. Brendon had several skin grafts, but I don't remember the details. My mother knows. I remember one of the nurses always put a cloth over my brother's penis when I was there. I was aware that this was something they did just for me, a small act of attention to the fourteen-year-old girl in the room. The nurse probably didn't think very much about this slight care she offered to me, but this one act made me feel seen, somehow. I felt seen and I liked that, but I also remember thinking it wasn't necessary, that my brother's penis wasn't going to traumatize me. The tub was a giant steel butterfly. It was used with the worst cases. I remember pain crossing my brother's face, just kind of flooding his face every now and then. I remember groans. I remember wanting to protect him from everything. And this hydrotherapy—you know they can only do it a few minutes at a time, right? Or it's too much. For anyone.

 escapes anger neighbors

Susan Braungart. Calgary Herald; Calgary, Alta. 07 Mar 1990: B3.

Neighbors of a Claresholm treatment centre for autistic adults are angry that they weren't told about two recent escapes from the centre.

Operators of the ██████

Ranch are supposed to notify nearby residents about escapes under an agreement with the Municipal District of Willow Creek.

Neighbors said…

One thing mom knows: there's no way in hell Brendon turned on a tap. She'll say that even the doctor said that at the time: there's no way in hell Brendon was laying in that bathtub and turned on the tap with either his hand or his feet. He was unable to move at the time, that's what a few of the workers from the place said when they called mom in the hospital, wanting to make right out of what was going on where they worked. The one man who worked there called and told mom how sick Brendon was, that he should have been in the hospital already. And then mom goes to the wound itself. No splash marks. The top of the burn ended evenly all around the leg. Looked like he was dipped in something, she always says.

The years he was at his safe place. Grabbing my hand Saturday morning when we walked in the weekends we drove down. Grabbing my hand and dragging me to the playroom. We never saw so many toys. Always one hand cupping one ear. Ah-da, ah-da, da-da-da.

There Were Things Going on We Knew Nothing About

VOICEOVER: Getting ▮▮▮▮▮▮ side of the story was very difficult. We arranged a time and showed up at The Ranch, but at the last minute we couldn't come to terms about what she would and wouldn't talk about.

▮▮▮▮: I cannot talk about anything that involves a client.

VOICEOVER: So to get a psychologist's perspective [book shown: Institutional Abuse of Children and Youth] we went to University of Alberta professor Dick Sobsie. His specialty: abuse at institutions. We showed Sobsie some hidden camera videotape we recorded at a ▮▮▮▮▮▮ bowling alley just last week. ▮▮▮▮ clients were there at a night out. We wanted to know what psychologists thought of an incident we saw there.

SOBSIE: Seems to me the client's already quiet and this guy [Ranch employee] seems to be right in his face almost trying to provoke something from him. See that seems troublesome to me. Seems like he's provoking the client and particularly the second person coming in and grabbing the client. It's totally inappropriate.

REPORTER: Is this abuse?

SOBSIE: They're using power inappropriately. And using power inappropriately is my definition of what abuse is. When I see two guys leaning on somebody, one of them going for their throat, I consider that to be more than just a breach of etiquette.

REPORTER: And if this is happening in public then...

SOBSIE: I would expect worse to happen in private.

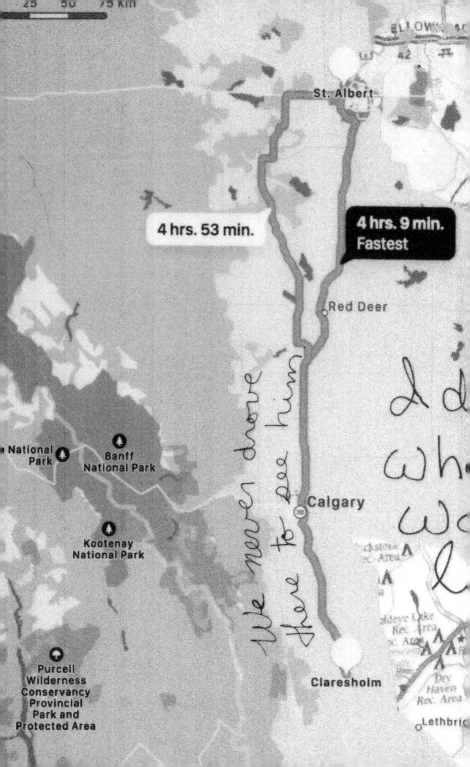

Wildwood

St. Albert

Claresholm

Options

4 hrs. 9 min.
442 km · Fastest route

4 hrs. 53 min.
492 km

don't know

at that drive

ould be

ike.

CHAPTER TEN

Traveling to See the Cousins in St. Norbert

He was too short for the bike our mother had gifted him.
And I couldn't tell for sure, but I thought he was pedalling
in the wrong direction. I'd inherited the family tradition of
moving on, but I hadn't been gifted with finding places.

The boy wanted his curses. So he pedalled through the
street, shedding his clothes until he was naked as the day he
was born, except for the near-invisible sash. Look at that
naked boy on the bicycle, people said as he passed. At home
in the evening, everyone who saw him told a story about him
then. And he was a different boy in each story.

The River's Seeds Will Wait in the Cone

They say that rivers are alive, that rivers change over time.
Seemed to me my mother changed after my brother was
injured. She survived by drying up and transforming herself
into a little Jack Pine, growing near the river of her mother's
memory. The resin in the Jack Pine tree's cones melts only
at crisis-high temperatures, so she was safe from what had
happened to her oldest son. At scorching temperatures, the

scales of the cone open up, and most of the seeds wait in the cone until the ground is ready—until it has cooled enough that the heat won't kill them—before they fall onto the ground. Survival brought the Jack Pine out of the river of my mother, and she waited for the seeds of her next life to drop; we each had to find our own riverbed, our own way to flow after that, if we could.

I've been dreaming about a Powwow I was at a couple of years ago and a woman who danced there. The Powwow happened out on the Prairies, where I hadn't been for years. In this dream, I always feel sated, as if I can stop roaming for a little while.

Every time I enter this dream, the dancing woman is dressed the way she was when I saw her in the round dance. She always wears a Métis sash draped over one shoulder and opposite hip and a ribbon skirt that is less colourful than those worn by most of the other women there. The stripes of this woman's sash are brighter than her skirt. In her one braid she wears a decoration in the shape of a beaded Métis infinity symbol.

In my dream, I am sometimes dancing, but more often I'm sitting in the grass watching the Powwow with the Elders and the children and the dancers waiting their turns. In the dream I have a book with me, and it is sometimes open on my lap as I sit in the grass with my legs stretched out straight ahead. It's a book by Chantal Fiola, one that I've been reading in my waking life, *Rekindling the Sacred Fire: Métis Ancestry and Anishinaabe Spirituality*. The book murmurs to me about the ways colonization separated Métis people from their ancestral spiritual ways. The people around me keep on dancing.

When she is dancing in the round, the woman some-times carries an eagle feather. With each dreaming her hair becomes more grey than it was in waking life, until there is almost no brown left at all. The book on my lap speaks as the people dance and the book gossips about of the impacts of missionaries and residential schools and the child welfare system. The book speaks at the same volume as the people's feet in the grass and I can't quite hear everything, but I make out uneven phrases about the way our colonial history created a disconnection between some Métis and their full culture, making it hard for them to feel they have a right to participate in ceremonies that were once a part of their ancestors' lives.

Many of the First Nations and Métis women and men wear medicine bags and leggings beaded with flowers in the Métis style, designs that call out their own celebrations in colour, line, and shape as the dancing goes on. Sometimes I leave my book in the grass and join the all-people's dances. This brings me joy that carries through to my waking life.

There is a moment each time I dream about her that the woman leaves the dance and I follow where she leads. She walks west in search of water and by the time I catch up and approach her, she is standing still with a water bottle in her hand. I tell her that I like her sash. I ask her if she is Métis. In the dream I am wearing jeans and a plain green T-shirt and my hair is its usual blonde. She looks at me without recognition even though she has been appearing in my dreams regularly. She nods and she says, Yes, I'm Métis. I'm full-blood Métis, she says.

The prairie sun is heavy on our foreheads. I feel how long I've been in the fog in Newfoundland and Labrador, where I've been trying to make a home. I squint against the bright heat. My body is still trying to recall how to be beside a prairie river, under a prairie sky, wrapped in that prairie smell. This woman's skin is paler than many here, but there are enough First Nation people here with skin both lighter and darker than hers, and there are enough Métis here with skin both lighter and darker than hers, that she doesn't stand out.

I am aware somehow that this is a dream, and I am amused that I have recreated the exact Powwow I was at a few years back. Some of the people here have come to this dream to dance. Some arrive in my dream to settle on blankets and watch others dance. Just don't take pictures, whoever you are, wherever your ancestors are from. Even in a dream, the dances aren't for taking pictures.

She looks around and sees a friend approaching from across the grass. She turns back to me. People think it's easy to get your Métis card, she says, but it's not. I nod, thinking of the genealogy book each member of my family keeps to document and prove our numerous relations.

In this dream, she doesn't guess that I might belong here. She doesn't guess that my close relations are from here, though they since dispersed in so many directions. The smell of the land offers to me the possibility that I could belong right there on that soil in a future summer or in another dream and that is enough for me.

The woman in my dream knows all about her story of belonging. I teach beading, she tells me. I teach drumming and dancing, she says. She offers a list of her relations and I smile. It's what so many Métis I've known do when they meet one another, even in a dream. Her relations are many and it takes some time. I hear a name and know that she is related to one of my ancestors, and so she is related to me. "Yes," she says again. "My people, we're full-blood Métis. And we chose the Indians. That's why I dance."

Her friend joins her and they return to their blanket to rest, drink water, and watch the dancers. I return to my book, which is murmuring still.

∞

Think of the traumas the buffalo survived, one after another. How they lived through the great ice age to lose almost everything to the pressure of the European markets. To lose all to a plan to starve Indigenous Peoples into submission, into signing treaties they wouldn't sign if the buffalo were numerous and thriving.

Bison home and migration patterns were pawns in European power struggles. Hunting became more difficult. For the Métis and other Indigenous hunters, this meant paying attention not just to environmental and land cues, but to keep abreast of who'd set fires in which places to stop the buffalo herds from migrating toward a Nation they wanted to keep submissive. That sort of thing.

In all these political maneuvers, follow the trails of the buffalo.

Louis recalls the year the remaining buffalo herds took "refuge" in the Cypress Hills. Over the years, Métis hunters had to travel farther and farther south in search of the remaining buffalo herds before they stopped hunting altogether. The buffalo were searching for a place to recuperate from their losses and to decide where they were going to go next.

Mama said those burns were like nothing she had ever seen in her life. She called it the room. She'd say, When they took him in to that room and had to peel that skin off. Then she'd trail off. Mama didn't know how Brendon could just lie in that stretcher and let them do it, even sedated as he was. They had to take some of the skin off his thigh to patch up his foot. And even now she'll say how the foot doesn't look good. They have to be really careful with his shoe because the skin is tender and breaks easily. Infection sets in and because Brendon can't understand how to take care, he'll end up in the hospital to get a few rounds of antibiotics. When she first saw the burns, they were raw and blistery and purple and all kinds of colours. Skin was peeling away from there and there was raw flesh and she'd never seen burns like that before. On one leg, the burns to just below his knee, even all around. And then on the thighs, there were cigarette burns, well, what she assumed was cigarettes because what else made burns like that, she couldn't think. On his privates, too.

Mom said the nurses explained that the care home's owner told them she was the guardian and that's why they didn't call his mom. The nurses told mom that ███████████ had said that mom didn't want anything to do with Brendon and that she never comes around to visit, so don't bother contacting his mom. The nurses couldn't believe it when mom phoned.

The Métis of Red River were effectively pushed off their land through the corrupt scrip system and the constant influx of new settlers coming in from Ontario. Some headed out to the northern United States, or further north in Manitoba, and many went westward, deeper into Canada. . . ."

—Chantal Fiola in *Rekindling the Sacred Fire*

There Were Things Going on We Knew Nothing About

VOICEOVER: We wanted to get more information on the Ranch. So we had a CBC researcher get a job there. David Smith lasted only two days at the Ranch. He came back to Edmonton and told us about the questionable treatment he saw. This was the worst incident.

SMITH: The second day at lunchtime Trevor Hoffman was feeding Kurt. Again. Alone. And I did not see what Kurt did to anger Trevor. What I saw was that Trevor picked him up and put his arm across Kurt's throat, put his hand on the back of Kurt's head and propelled him into the wall head first. It was loud. It was hard.

This is the same Trevor Hoffman convicted of assault. Last summer he kicked a client in the face. As of last week Hoffman was still working at the Ranch.

[NOTE: EPISODE AIRED IN 1993]

Some of the new complex post-traumatic stress disorder resources suggest that animals don't hold onto trauma the way humans do. Healing for humans, they say, involves letting our bodies return to the animalistic state during which fear, emotion, and trauma are processed and released, not remembered. When healing, humans can access this non-human emotional processing. Like a deer. When attacked a deer plays dead. If the attacker leaves it alive, the animal lays still for some time, twitching, releasing the stress through muscle movement. The deer gets up after that, seemingly untroubled and unchanged by the event. I don't know. If you've ever seen an abused dog, you'll know that theory only goes so far on the individual level. And at the group level or the species level? And the cultural level? They don't talk about that.

He was such a slim child. Pulling my hand, as if to say come with me. One hand cupping one ear. Ah-da, ah-da, da-da-da. I always went, you know, back then I always followed in his wake.

Centre's cleared of charge

Eva Ferguson. Calgary Herald; Calgary, Alta. 03 April 1990.

A provincial investigation has cleared a Claresholm treatment centre of allegations of neglect in connection with an incident in which an autistic youth suffered third-degree burns to his feet.

An earlier investigation by Claresholm RCMP into the scalding of 18-year-old Brendon Porter at the ▮▮▮ Ranch concluded that no criminal charges would be laid.

Police said the burns were the result of the youth acci-dentally turning the hot water on while he was in the bathtub.

...There were also allegations that Porter had suffered cigarette burns. "As far as we're concerned there were never any cigarette burns, and the government's statement that the injuries were accidental confirms that," said ▮▮▮▮▮.

...Sharon Williams, a former employee of the Ranch who complained about conditions there, said the investigation ignored the facts.

The prairie dog's fussiness is part of a treaty.

Long ago the land wanted to become the Prairies. So the land made an agreement with this small animal. It asked the animal to let loose its compulsive tendencies and to use its talent for neurosis. It asked the prairie dog to de-clutter its yard and obsessively tidy up.

Does this mesquite bush give me joy? For the prairie dog, the answer is almost always a no. What in humans might be diagnosed as an anxiety disorder, becomes essential to creation.

Prairie dogs want to be able to see far and wide so they can watch for predators. It's about risk assessment, really. Bushes and trees get in the way of proper security. So, prairie dogs become aggressive gardeners, removing anything that grows taller than they can stand on their hind feet.

The mesquite shrub grows taller than this.

Grasslands can't tolerate this woody shrub. Mesquite pushes deep roots into the earth and sucks up water, drying everything out in an ecosystem defined by lack of water. By chewing up the roots or sucking on the stems, prairie dogs kill all the mesquite in the area and keep the desert away, leaving both the grasslands and themselves content.

Prairie dogs can't stop fussing over their underground homes. They build elaborate dens and, in the process, break up hard-baked desert soil, making it better for growing grassland plants and for foraging. They've been called the architect of North America's grasslands, a grand name for an anxious little bundle of fur. Their grazing shapes the plant life in the area in such a way that it creates unique, impossible to replicate habitat for grassland birds, such as the prairie chicken, mountain plovers, killdeer, and McCown's longspurs. Their burrows provide refuge for other species who need a space to temporarily escape from predators, storms, or extreme temperatures.

So, the nervous edginess of the little prairie dog is as important to the grasslands as is the solid, steady movements of herds of buffalo.

But the prairie dog is not essential to the new way of life on the Prairies. Where land is converted for farming and cattle ranching, the prairie dog is inconvenient. Farmers and ranchers saw the animal as a pest, believing the animal competed with cows and horses for grass and grazing land and that the prairie dog had no right to its burrows and its gardening. Prairie dogs were eradicated from 98 per cent of the land they called home. The treaty between grassland and buffalo and prairie dog was broken.

Once a treaty is broken, there's all kinds of trust that needs to be built back up, all kinds of details need to be worked over again and again, and you need a somewhat annoying, fussy, detail-oriented little mammal to lay the groundwork and support the negotiations that will never really end, not as long as there are people living on the land.

The story isn't over because any effort to return the buffalo to the land and to restore and protect our grasslands needs the prairie dog. So, a lot of organizations and conservationists are working with this little animal, working on a new treaty that builds a trail and starts a journey to the grasslands of the future.

∞

You were angry. You've told me that a few times, when I called you to ask you what you remember. I keep asking about it because it seems so strange, that emotion.

I wasn't angry.

How could they do that to our brother? Sure, I asked that all the time, with every waking breath, with every thought. I kept asking that question in the hospital and back at school, where I told no one what had happened and where no one asked why I was away.

You know, I think that I turned my fury against myself. I wish I'd had your ability to feel anger outward then.

I ran dry. I didn't know it until just now, honest I didn't.

I told you I called one of his workers from back then, didn't I? All those years ago, I didn't know to look for the helpers.

∞

How a River Changes Direction

It's not the volume of water that changes the direction of a river's flow, that bends a river to a new direction, east or west. It's the rocks the shores are made of. It's the rocks that bend a river and it's also the rocks that hold to their position against everything the water flings at them.

Bison turn up bones of their ance
wallowing spots in return

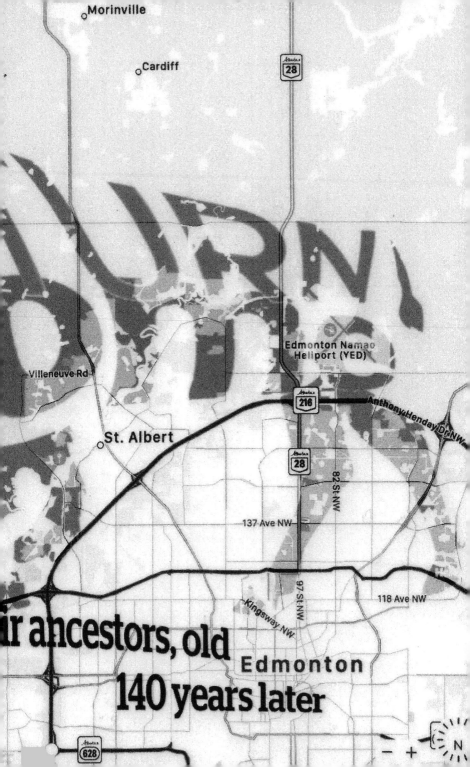

CHAPTER ELEVEN

Fire on the Prairies

As he traveled away, the boy met a doctor who was crossing the street. You're going the wrong way, the doctor said. The boy kept on pedalling. He watched a whippoorwill in the sky. The whippoorwill, who was far from home himself, called to the boy on the ground, you're going the wrong way. The boy kept on pedalling. He pedalled and pedalled and pedalled until he came upon a buffalo, who was creating a wallow in a quiet cul-de-sac. Brendon didn't speak, so he got off his bicycle and he reached out to touch the thick hair on it's back. The buffalo looked at him. You aren't going to the river, are you? the buffalo asked. Brendon shook his head. And why should you? Get on my back. Brendon left his bicycle there and climbed on the buffalo's back. The buffalo spoke again. I was looking for a home and a family, said the buffalo. Brendon buried his face in the buffalo's fur. It made him smile.

What the Riverbed Is Made of

I was near to running dry. I didn't dare release the flood that was bursting. I let myself trickle to such a tiny flow nobody would notice me. Our brother's life, it kept on moving on, finding the easiest way between here and there, creating falls that cascaded into a future he couldn't control, but he let himself fall all the same. A waterfall moves upstream throughout a river's life. It's not because of the strength of the river's flow. The waterfall moves because of what its riverbed is made of.

Tragedy adds to ▇▇▇▇ woes

Patty Fuller. Alberta Report.
Vol. 20 Issue 17, p12. Dec. 4, 1993.

Details a drowning incident at Claresholm's ▇▇▇ Ranch in Canada…

I went with mom to visit him at the Alberta Hospital in Edmonton a few times. This was when he was an adult, when he was in between homes, before the home he's in today. Mom remembers that as the place he was most happy. Because of all the glass windows in the long hallway. He could just walk back and forth and pace and pace and look and look. That's what he likes, she'll say with an edge of pride in her voice, that's what makes him happy. Just leave him alone and let him pace. If she keeps talking about the Alberta Hospital, she'll mention how they took him off all his medication there for a while. He was just shaking and shaking. He'd cross his arms and tilt his body way back, looking up. That scared mama, really scared her. He's been on medications too long, mom says. He goes funny off his meds. But once they put him back on his meds, he stopped shaking and he straightened his posture again and he was happy there.

∞

Louis Goulet is about nine years old, and he is traveling with his parents with an organized caravan of Métis families in search of buffalo.

> *By the time we got to Beaver River we were already*
> *worried about prairie fires cutting into the grazing*
> *land we needed along the way, so we veered off a*
> *little in the direction of Moose Jaw.... After about*
> *a week of slow and difficult marching, the smoke*
> *rose, indicating either that the fire was no longer in*
> *the peat or that the wind had changed direction....*
> *Our guess was soon confirmed.*
>
> —Louis Goulet, *Vanishing Spaces*

Mom visited the Ranch before she placed him there. She liked it. Well, as much as she'd like any place like that, she'll add. I remember her enthusiasm. I remember her describing the therapy the owner said she planned for Brendon. Mama had this hope in her face. One of the main stipulations, one of the only things they asked of mom, was for her not to visit. That he needed time to settle in and to look to the owner as his teacher. No contact with anybody who knows him, for a number of months, at least. That's why she hadn't been down there. Nobody had.

There Were Things Going on We Knew Nothing About

REPORTER: Our investigation has renewed the government's interest in the ███ Ranch. Sources within the social services tell us that the Minister Mike Cardinal made a visit last weekend. They say he wasn't impressed by what he saw. That he has asked his staff for a plan to move residents out and to shut the Ranch down. For CBC News, I'm ██████████ in Edmonton.

∞

Mom called the cops from the hospital. They came in to examine Brendon. When they went out to the property where the facility Brendon had been burned on was, the owner of the Ranch met the cops with her lawyer. They weren't allowed to set foot on the property for so many hours. The cops said there wasn't any point in going in there by then because everything's cleared up and there'd be no sign of anything wrong.

There's No Way to Control a River

Like my brother, I only wanted to get away from here and go there and I leaned into the easiest route. We want to believe what we leave behind will stay in the place we first found it, and that's the reason we try to control rivers. But there's really no way to do it.

∞

> *The council didn't show it, but they were worried.*
> *Scouts sent out on reconnaissance were beating*
> *the flames and lighting small blazes to change the*
> *currents of air rushing to feed the main fire. They*
> *reported to the council that the fire was running*
> *along a big ridge that snaked between two muskegs.*

—Louis Goulet, *Vanishing Spaces*

∞

Without water, grasslands lose their knowledge base. The stories passed from grass to soil tell how to let water in, how to let life in, again and again, into the soil so it doesn't all slip away. Water's stories tell how to provide a bed, a base, a source for the flow of rivers and streams. How to flood and how to parch.

Without intact grasslands, the Prairies struggle with the biggest water security issues in Canada. Without those grasslands, there's always too much water and too little water at the wrong times. Downstream from disturbed, converted, or redacted grassland there is increased runoff from cropland, carrying excess nutrient loads from fertilizer and chemicals. There's floods, like the ones in recent years in Manitoba. There's nothing to hold the water in and during the spring rains, there's too much and the ground can't soak it up. In the summer, the grass isn't there to share the water it keeps in the earth, so the soil dries up and, without an underground source flow, the rivers run themselves to a trickle.

One hand cupping one ear: ah-da, ah-da, da-da-da. I always went, you know, back then.

One of the front-line care workers became particularly close to Brendon. When new staff couldn't get him to cooperate, they'd go find her. The bathtub was always an issue. He often refused to come out. It got to where she could stand out in the hallway and say, Brendon, what are you doing? And then he'd come running out of the bath and laugh at her. It took a while, she said, but he was just one of those kids that formed a bond. It'd make her laugh. Sometimes, if she was working with one of the other kids, he'd sit beside her on the couch as if to say, you're my person and you're not supposed to be working with anybody else.

∞

> *...they'd practised manoeuvres to assure that the*
> *carts could be quickly and efficiently harnessed*
> *and moved in the direction of any sloughs that had*
> *water enough to protect them from the flames.*

—Louis Goulet, *Vanishing Spaces*

Oldring failed autistics

Editorial. *Edmonton Journal (Edmonton, Alberta, Canada) ·*
1 Feb 1993, Mon · Page 6

...A lot of dedicated professionals tried very hard to do something to help the 22 residents at Ranch, but Oldring wasn't one of them.... For the sake of silent men, locked in a frightening world of their own, he could have risked court action and negative publicity on the hunch that time would prove him right. He chose to do nothing...

And what would happen if we let grassland build its relations with us, let it live the life it wants? Academic studies have been answering this question using numbers to describe the relationship between grassland and water security. One of these studies, titled *Quantifying the Environmental Benefits of Conserving Grassland*, concluded that keeping just some grassland intact would prevent almost two trillion gallons of surface runoff from entering the Mississippi River water basin each year. A small portion of intact grassland within the water system studied prevented 46 million tons of sediment, 87 million pounds of phosphorus and 427 million pounds of nitrogen from running off and getting into the water.

Together, grasslands and water systems give life to the urban landscapes that rely on them. The cities are disconnected from the land around them, so they don't know where their water comes from.

On the Prairies the tall grass holds the water in tight to the soil and it's an ancient treaty everybody used to understand. Water is sacred and the grass, well, everyone knew that grass is responsible for water.

When the crier had given the order for the wagons to drive into the water in the sloughs, it was done without a word. Once the fire had passed, the same order prevailed, in reverse. No sooner were the wagons out of the water than the oxen were unhitched in the glow of retreating flames. Not long after, the first light of dawn appeared. An hour later, the tents were pitched and everybody bedded down except for the guards...

—Louis Goulet, *Vanishing Spaces*

The future of

Morris River

for mov two on

Grand

Second St

Lucinda St N

Charles St W

-4°

ture of this

place is not

on the map

Road 330

Highway 75 Frontage Rd

Riverview Dr

75

Morris River

Jubilee St

Grandin

Second St

Lucinda St N

Kennedy St W

Mulvey St

Mulvey St E

James St

Charles St W

Charles St E

N

CHAPTER TWELVE

Buffalo Treaty

The name of a river is the second word in the book *Vanishing Spaces*. Of course it is. Louis Goulet and his family made a life along rivers that flowed through land that is part of today's map of Canada. But they weren't in Canada yet, not then.

The signatories to the Buffalo Treaties of 2014 and 2019 include: Blackfeet Nation, Blood Tribe, Siksika Nation, Piikani Nation, the Assiniboine and Gros Ventre Tribes of Fort Belknap Indian Reservation, the Assiniboine and Sioux Tribes of Fort Peck Indian Reservation, the Salish and Kootenai Tribes of the Confederated Salish and Kootenai Indian Reservation, Tsuu T'ina Nation, and the Nakoda Nation. It's beginning: more treaties will be created to bring the bison back to heal all our land.

∞

■■■■■ RESIDENTS RELOCATED: *[Final Edition]*

Chris Dawson. *Calgary Herald;*
Calgary, Alta. 10 Feb 1993: B4. Page 6

OWNER VOWS TO REFUSE INSPECTION

The owner of a home for autistic adults has relocated her residents in accordance with provincial regulations and isn't breaking any laws, she claims.

And ■■■■■■■■■■■■, who operates the controversial ■■■ Ranch near ■■■■■■, said Tuesday she won't allow a provincial licensing inspector to go through the buildings today...

Still, the land claim and conservation dance everyone's got to learn is a crooked one, like the dance we call the Red River Jig. There's traditional parts to the jig, the steps everyone repeats because they build connections. And there's the new parts, too, the steps improvised depending on what works in the moment and what speaks to what's going on in your corner of the stage.

∞

Coalition of northern Metis communities file historic land claim

Amanda Short SASKATOON STAR-PHOENIX
OCTOBER 17, 2019

The first-of-its-kind inter-provincial land claim is for an area of about 122,000 square kilometres. Plaintiffs are looking to redress the scrip system, a government-run land claim process for Metis people that took place throughout the late 1800s and early 1900s.

… "This is a long overdue action that could have been avoided if successive governments had simply done the right thing and admitted the scrip process deprived Metis people of what the law promised to us…"

North West Land Claims & Other Related MNS Land Claims

Agenda
1. Métis Connection to Land
2. Métis & Section 35, Constitution Act, 1982
3. Northwest Saskatchewan Métis Land Claim
4. 2019 Land Claim
5. Land Claims Policy
6. Current Status & Next Steps

> — a slide from a presentation by Métis Nation of Saskatchewan legal representative on Feb, 28, 2020, titled "Connection to Land."

I often think the Red River Jig (Oayâche Mannin)
was invented on evenings like that when sometimes
the only instrument was an Indian drum.
....That's why the winter life on the far prairies of
the west was so attractive to those folks who lived
by the plains, for the plains, and nothing else. They
were absolutely free to lead their own lives and
hang on to the old ways of their land.

—Louis Goulet, *Vanishing Spaces*

My big brother taking me by the hand, pulling me into his world. One hand cupping one ear. Tapping a wall, a tree. A big smile. In a sing-song voice: da-da-da, and da-da-da again. Off I went with him.

One of the workers told me how she's thought about my brother over the years. How they do a lot with picture communication with nonverbal kids now. They give the kids books of images or even iPads with pictures so they can point to the pictures that express what they want or what they're thinking. She's thought sometimes that this kind of approach might have made a difference for Brendon. He could have shown everybody what he wanted. She always thought our brother had lots and lots to say, he just didn't have a great way to say it. They were always trying to read his mind.

...on the Missouri River. The dance started. There
was no wood floor and I don't remember any other

instruments than an Indian drum. Some men were
sitting on the ground around the drum, pounding
away like mad to the rhythm of the Red River Jig
while the dancing men and women took turns with
wild enthusiasm....
Broken by pauses when we sang, the dancing went
on into the wee hours of the morning.

—Louis Goulet, *Vanishing Spaces*

Brendon's younger sister had to learn how to burn. For the berries and the prairie dog and the grasses, she burned. She burned as a ceremonial invitation to herds of beautiful bison. She set fire to everything as a kind of reconciliation. For her children and her grandchildren. And for herself, that, too.

I called our brother's old school to ask about a woman I remembered who worked with Brendon when he was a child. They passed me to another one of his childhood workers, a woman who said she'd help if she could. She asked, "how is Brendon?" and I repeated to her what my mom always says, that he's as good as he can be. I don't know why I repeated to Brendon's old teacher exactly what my mom had said to me for years when I hadn't had a chance to fly back home to visit. He's as good as he can be. These past couple of years though, that's changed. Now when I phone, mom's happier and she says he's good, oh, he's good.

The woman on the phone wanted to talk about Brendon. She told me stories of a child who knew how to make everyone love him. That the aides who worked with him, all of them developed a steady affectionate bond with him. She emailed pictures of him at the school from thirty years ago, and there he was, surrounded by workers and other residents; smiling in one picture; accepting a holiday gift in another; and beaming while eating dinner at a table beside a young woman who worked with him. Happy. Loved. He belonged.

This is the same story told by the laughter and affection shown by the people who work with him in his group home now. All of them immigrants from other countries, all of them with so much to give to our brother and eager to have us visit. It took me a while to see what was in front of me, how each of those beautiful, complicated workers love our brother. This is the story our brother hasn't been able to tell us.

But he told it anyway, didn't he? Eventually, I mean. He told it through his connection to this woman, through his talent for being remembered, and through the love he'd inspired in this woman who worked part-time with him to get through school, this woman who became a psychologist because of her work with him. Don't you love that? Doesn't knowing that change everything?

"Le Metis"

> ...the MMF (Manitoba Metis Federation) remains
> in a partnership to maintain a herd of bison in
> Rosa, MB.... We plan to raise the herd...for food
> cultural and educational purposes...

> —from the MMF newsletter, "Le Metis"

Where a River Used to Be

Walk along a dry riverbed if you ever get the chance. Move time around a bit either way, forward or backward, and there's a river spreading herself out from one side of the riverbed to the other.

∞

The best way to find the burdock is to scout roadsides, ditches, waste areas, creek beds, pastures, and anywhere the earth has been disturbed. In the wild, burdock grows on injured soil. It flowers late in the summer, producing a seed head that matures into a burr.

It draws nutrients from deep within the ground and replenishes and heals the earth as it grows. When burdock is used as a medicine it works the same way, encouraging the body to restore the conditions necessary for healing.

That's how her brother found the buffalo who was looking for home. She's his sister, younger by five years. She likes to think that she watches out for everyone, her brother and the buffalo. But, all these years after she left home, it's still her brother and his buffalo looking out for her.

The highway between us and our brother. That's where we lived our lives. And our brother waiting for us then. Did it seem that way to you? Can't you see him standing with his forehead pressed against the window looking out of the home he lives in today? I can hear him as if we were there, now, pulling open the door to the home he's been living in for years, an affectionate worker at his side. You and me, our brother and sister, mom and whoever else has married in, whoever else belongs to us for the moment. Maybe our brother will vocalize his excitement in the way he always used to do, with one hand cupped over an ear and the other hand gently tapping a nearby surface. Watching us arrive, watching us leave. Tap, tap, tap, tap. Our brother, he waited for us.

until my hands
were numb
with cold

Skated here.

unsharpened blade

fell
got

my b

m

fell down
got back up

y brother?

My brother was
just outside
claresholm

Afterword

In the early months of 2021, my mother sent me a copy of a poem I'd written about my brother when I was fourteen. I'd written it while we were staying near the hospital and caring for him. Somehow, I'd lost my own tattered copy of the poem.

At that time, I'd already written this book and was working out how to approach edits and rewrites. I thought re-reading the poem could provide some insight into the mind of fourteen-year-old me. I didn't expect that poem to change the way I thought of my own role in this story.

Many writers and scholars have grappled with the process of telling a story that involves someone who cannot tell their own story. Brendon cannot tell his story. For that reason, the weight of this story rests on the shoulders of a fourteen-year-old girl who experiences trauma through witnessing what has happened to her brother. There are other possible ways to tell Brendon's story. No approach would be perfect, in part because his voice is missing. It is a large gap, but it is also a real-life gap, and an important one to stay with in this life story. I purposefully chose not to project my own voice or a created or imagined voice onto Brendon. Instead, I told the story through the eyes of his younger sister, myself—but also through the stagnated emotional experience of the fourteen-year-old girl I was. In focusing on the relationships between brother-sister, mother-daughter, and sister-sister, I told the story in the traditional Métis way, through a focus on connections and what those connections bring to the story and to the characters. We are only understood in the context of our relations.

With that in mind, the fragmentation and the bursts of storytelling purposefully mirror the psychological response to a trauma that was witnessed by a fourteen-year-old girl—and this witnessing became a trauma itself. Trauma fragments memory and fragments experiences. For the girl struggling to tell the story, there is no linear way to build the story into a comforting narrative arc. Although the story is about Brendon, it is also about the journey of his sister, who has to cope with his trauma and can find no resolution in talking it through with her brother as they get older or in hearing him tell his story. In fact, a key revelation in the story that does bring a sense of hope is the sister's realization as an adult many years later that the brother has been able to recover and move on—though she could never talk to him about it. All those years, it was Brendon's sister—myself—who continued to see the events through the eyes of trauma. This complexity is the result of the relational focus.

Scratching River might make a reader uncomfortable. Discomfort and even horror are both appropriate responses to a story about the abuse of mentally disabled people. It is the horror that the fourteen-year-old felt and the horror that trapped her in trauma for many years. As a writer, I did not feel the need to censor the horror, though I did decide to tell it "crooked," or sideways, through newspaper accounts. Indeed, there is so much to be gained from refusing to soften the sharpness in the family's unsuccessful attempts to get accountability. The acceptance of this stymied attempt at justice is one of the first steps toward healing. We do not gain anything by only reading and writing stories about victims of abuse that reframe being victimized as an opportunity to become empowered, particularly for a person with the kinds of mental illness that Brendon has.

Much of the detail about what happened to Brendon is offered up in the news stories. This narrative decision was a conscious one, made for many reasons. The news stories are in one sense measured and balanced. There is little sensationalizing in those stories. In fact, the objective, measured, and balanced approach of the articles invokes its own injustice. The use of the news stories mirrors the way the children (myself and my brother and sisters) found out about many of the details and it reflects their own inability to get their questions answered. It steers away from over-sentimentalizing details and from weaving my subjective interpretation into what happened to him and to other young men like him. Rather than sensationalizing, the stories tell it plain and offer a point of view steeped in a sense of balance that is almost certainly too much, given the details of what happened. In redacting specific names and details in the news stories, I evoke the kinds of memory gaps trauma can create and a sense of what can become unspeakable as a result of a fear of legal action.

I should let you know that I didn't intend to write about my brother. I intended to write a collection of responses to an oral history of an ancestor, who grew up traveling the Métis trails and following the buffalo on a Red River cart. My auntie Dale had asked me to get myself a copy of the book. I'd been visiting and she'd looked everywhere in her house for the book until she remembered she'd leant it to someone else. But get it, she said. He's our ancestor, she said. He's amazing, she said.

When I returned to my home in Newfoundland and Labrador I googled and found a used copy for sale from a bookseller in the United States, translated into English from its original French. I ordered a copy and in a month's time I had it in my hand: *Vanishing Spaces: Memoirs of Louis Goulet.* I'll always feel a debt to Louis Goulet—not only for telling his story, but for telling it with so much skill, humour, and even love.

As I read and wrote and took notes about Louis's life of traveling the Prairies and of the movement of goods and people by Métis along these routes between what are now two countries, I found myself re-experiencing flashbacks of my own childhood traveling the Prairies. Our reasons for travel were quite different, of course, at least on the surface. And yet my mind kept making the case for a less casual connection between our travels. I'd experience brief flashes of our near constant road trips to one place or another for one reason or another. It didn't seem to matter why to my mother, really, just that we were on the road on our way to somewhere else. My mother was at her best planning for the next place and telling stories about where she'd been and where we were going. She still is, though illness has slowed her quite a bit.

I wanted the stories and the different time periods to stand alongside each other not because the stories or their details in any way mirror each other, but because they share the same sky and the same Métis Nation. By placing these stories against each other I am saying that the details of our people's struggles change across time but that if we look closely, we will see that their sources of strength and their ability to survive are constant. We continue and we thrive when we recover our ability to tell our stories from the land seven generations back, pointing them in the direction of the seven generations that are coming ahead of us all. We survive because we are always moving and we bring our stories along.

As I read about Louis Goulet, the fourteen-year-old girl I was leaned over my shoulder. She began having a conversation with Louis Goulet and his story. How do you write a conversation like that? I couldn't. I did record their conversations, however, in the form of the series of memory maps included as part of the book.

Louis Goulet's oral history detailed deep cultural change and ecological grief, yet it is also a story about survival and of hope. Louis Goulet brought the fourteen-year-old to a time when he and his people grieved for the injustice and the loss that the Métis people were suffering. And yet, they found a way to walk the old paths in one way or another, at one time for the buffalo, then to transport and sell goods, and then for all kinds of work and to visit family and sites of cultural importance, maybe in carts and maybe in cars or in Greyhound buses.

What do Louis Goulet and my brother have to do with each other? They have little in common. My brother never followed the bison, never rode in the back of a Red River cart as a child, my brother never spoke Michif or French, he could never speak the names of any of the prairie birds Louis Goulet described in any language, though I'm certain my brother has his own words for the birds that fly into and out of the trees during his daily walks. Louis Goulet is a distant ancestor. Yet, they are connected in this book through my imagination and the similar way each of their stories impacts me, teaching me how to heal, how to move on.

Louis Goulet's oral history is not the story of the end of anything. His story recounts struggle and transition for the Métis people, but his story is just the beginning. If my brother taught me how to heal from what happened to him in the twentieth century, Louis Goulet taught me how to heal from what happened to my ancestors over many centuries. Louis taught me how to travel back to Manitoba and what to look for in the land. His oral history taught me how to see the trails he'd travelled and to see how he kept travelling toward the future. He taught me how to cope with fire and how to set traditional fires so that the bison will return and the prairie grass will grow tall. He taught me how to recognize the resurgence of his people, of my people, and he taught me how to see the Métis rise again and again. And he taught me that my place in all of this might be similar to his. I could tell my story. Just tell it, and let it flow to where it needed to go.

The act of writing one's story is incredibly powerful; it is like being swept up in a strong current. I am not the same person I was. There is a purity in the fragmented nature of this manuscript that I can't return to. It was written as I was uncovering the shards. I hadn't begun piecing any of it together. I didn't have any story for the teenage rage and grief that shook me to my core. This manuscript is honest and jagged. Now, when I try to return to edit or tinker with the manuscript, I bring the healing I've worked for as well as the broad understanding of the fuller narrative in which my stories and my brother's stories live. And because I now bring all this with me, I can't return to those months when my memories of this time knocked me over as I as writing them. I can't tell it like it was then because it is no longer like that.

My mother sent me the poem I wrote. I wondered if there was anything in that poem that would be relevant to editing this manuscript. I'd written that poem in the evenings after spending days in the hospital with my mother and brother. The poem is called "Wild Man" because I thought of my brother as this man who was free from having to do what was expected of him. It was something I admired fiercely. Caring for him in the hospital after his burn injuries, I was seeing him at his worst, and the poem I wrote tells the story of a boy who, to my eyes, was giving up. Reading the poem now, I read the love for my brother and the admiration for his ability to make me laugh all the time and the grief I felt at the loss of those things. At the time, I didn't know it was temporary. It seemed to me he would never recover. It seemed that way to my mother, too, and her grief and anger were overwhelming.

All these years later, I read something else in that poem, too. In the words I wrote, I read the beginning what I now understand to be a long-lasting depression, one that I tried to suppress, one I buried. When my brother recovered enough to leave the hospital, he was welcomed back to his child-hood school and home where the workers who'd known him and loved him for ten years nursed him, cared for him, and brought him back to himself. I went back to our apartment and our next move and the next, and yet I remained stuck in the hospital, unable to see his recovery. His retreat from life did not last. Mine, for many reasons, did. The process of writing this book has been the process of offering that four-teen-year-old girl another way to see what happened, of meet-ing her right in the darkness where she was at, offering her support and empathy and, most importantly, opening up that crevice where hope had been buried. My brother survived and healed and learned to trust again. And so can that fourteen-year-old girl. All she ever needed was for me to put a hand on her shoulder and tell her it'll be okay. Something like healing will come in time.

A bibliography can be dangerous terrain.

Relations

Brendon, my brother. *Teaching by example.* All our lives.

Donita and Dale, my mother and auntie. *Nurturing the connections to our Métis family history and all the stories.* All our lives.

Colleen, my younger sister. *Storyteller and memory keeper.* All our lives.

Louis Goulet, ancestor. *Storyteller and memory keeper.* Told his story and allowed it to be recorded for the book, *Vanishing Spaces: Memoirs of Louis Goulet* (Original French title: *L'espace de Louis Goulet*), for future generations so that we can return to the Prairies through your eyes and your stories.

Estelle and Olive Goulet, my grandmother and her sister. Fiddle, piano, spoons, and performance, *The Red River Echoes.* All their lives.

Bob Goulet. Fiddle, *The Red River Echoes.* All his life.

Chris Sheridan. *Family Tree.* Family Historian.

wahkohtowin, all my ancestors who established a new Nation along the Red River and the diaspora and descendants of the Métis people who created our prairie homeland and who now live all over the world.

Note: I'm living here in Newfoundland and Labrador, but I'm always there with you all in heart and mind and soul.

> *A bibliography makes fence posts from publication years and names.*
> *A bibliography wants to border.*
> *The bibliographies I like to read are incomplete and will vanish in a moment.*

Home: land I've learned from, places I've lived

The Goulet river lots. *The Red River*. Co-created our people; all the teachings began in collaboration with this land, that sky and the network of rivers that sang there.

> *A bibliography tempts me.*
> *A bibliography wants to be the apple.*
> *In place of a bibliography I propose something else.*
> *In its place, a river.*

Métis storytellers and artists who've shared works from which I've learned, an incomplete list

Bob Goulet, for the music that led me here. Maria Campbell, for inviting me in. Lisa Bird-Wilson, for the stories you write that remind me of my connections and for reading early drafts. Marilyn Dumont. Katherena Vermette. Cherie Dimaline, for your vision of the future. Tenille Campbell, because your poetry upends all my expectations. Beatrice Mosionier. Jesse Thistle, for writing us all back home. Christi Belcourt, for showing us the layers in beauty. Warren Cariou. Chelsea Vowel. Lee Maracle. Leah Marie Dorion. Gregory Scofield, because you knew two Métis women. Louis Goulet, for your stories.

All my mother's ancestors: *Goulet, Siveright, Bouchard, Genthon, Marion, and many more.* Generations of their lives inscribed on the land I belong to.

Belcourt, Christie. *Medicines to Help Us: Traditional Métis Plant Use.* Gabriel Dumont Institute, 2007.

Birdsell, Sandra. *Waiting For Joe.* Random House Canada, 2010.

Bird-Wilson, Lisa. *Just Pretending.* Coteau Books, 2013.

Campbell, Maria. *Halfbreed.* Goodread Biography, 1983.

Campbell, Tenille. *#IndianLovePoems.* McNally Robinson. 2017.

———. *nedi nezu (Good Medicine).* Arsenal Pulp Press. 2021.

Cariou, Warren. *Lake of the Prairies.* Doubleday Canada. 2002.

Dimaline, Cherie. *The Girl Who Grew a Galaxy.* Theytus Books, 2013.

———. *The Marrow Thieves.* DCB, 2017.

Dorion, Leah Marie. *Featured Artworks Gallery.* https://www.leahdorion.ca/gallery.html

Dumont, Marilyn. *The Pemmican Eaters.* ECW Press, 2015.

———. *That Tongued Belonging.* Kegedonce Press, 2007.

Goulet, Bob. *The Red River Jig.* https://tunearch.org/wiki/Red_River_Jig [accessed June 29, 2021].

Goulet, Louis. Oral history in *Vanishing Spaces: Memoirs of Louis Goulet, collected by Guillaume Charette and translated by Ray Ellenwood.* Editions Bois-Brulets, 1980.

Monsionier, Beatrice. *In Search of April Raintree.* Highwater Press, 2016.

Scofield, Gregory. *I Knew Two Métis Women.* Polestar, 2000.

———. *Louis: Heretic Poems.* Nightwood Editions, 2011.

———. *Thunder Through My Veins.* Anchor Canada, 2019.

————. *Witness, I Am.* Nightwood Editions, 2016.

Thistle, Jesse. *From the Ashes: My Story of Being Métis, Homeless, and Finding My Way.* Simon and Schuster Canada, 2019.

Vermette, Katherena. *North End Love Songs.* The Muses' Company, 2012.

Vowel, Chelsea. *Indigenous Writes: A Guide to First Nations, Métis, & Inuit Issues in Canada.* HighWater Press. 2016.

————. "You're Métis? So Which of Your Parents Is an Indian?" Web log post. âpihtawikosisân. WordPress, 20 Dec., 2011 https://apihtawikosisan.com/2011/12/youre-metis-so-which-of-your-parents-is-an-indian/

I want to create a bibliography in the likeness of a herd of bison. Calves and mothers at the centre.

I want my bibliography to meander. I want my bibliography to wallow. I want my bibliography with a thick coat of hair, a strong rump, and a tall hump.

I want to create a bibliography that nourishes the grassland and supports an ecosystem.

This is where I begin. This is my first step.

Home: land I've learned from, places I've lived

Treaty 1 territory in Manitoba, the heart. St. Albert, for a few years. Alberta. The Goulet river allotments, still marked out on old surveys. Rennie and all the other little official and unofficial communities in which my great grandfather and grandmother lived. Chilliwack. Cultus Lake.

The mountain forests I walked in for hours alone. The grasslands I walked through, reverent, and silent. The place where the sun, the grass and the air combine to make that smell, you know what I mean. That yearling bear I ran into.

Saint John and St. John's. St. Albert. Alberta. Treaty 1 territory in Manitoba, the heart of the Métis Nation.

Don't eat before reading a bibliography.
You'll get cramps.

Métis scholars, researchers and teachers I've learned from so far

Maria Campbell, for the fierce history. Joshua Morin, for the language. Lawrence Barkwell, for the beading and the stories, among so many other things. Marilyn Dumont, for the poetry. Katherena Vermette, your stories still make me cry. Chris Sheridan, for keeping our history safe and for laughing at me until I laugh at myself. Dale Hunter, for your teachings and your love. Jennifer Adese, for a path into the future. Lee Maracle, for telling me how to find the path beneath my feet. Chantal Fiola. George R.D. Goulet, for your work and your gracious welcome. Brenda Macdougall, for your maps.

Adese, Jennifer. Spirit gifting: Ecological knowing in Métis life narratives. *Decolonization: Indigeneity, Education & Society* 3(3), 2015, pp. 48–66.

Barkwell, Lawrence, Dorion, Leah, Prefontaine, Darren. *Resources for Métis Researchers.* Winnipeg: Louis Riel Institute of the Manitoba Métis Federation. Gabriel Dumont Institute of Native Studies and Applied Research, 1999.

Campbell, Maria. *Halfbreed.* Goodread Biography, 1983.

Dumont, Marilyn, ed. *Initiations: A selection of young Native writings.* Theytus Books, 2007.

Fiola, Chantal. *Rekindling the Sacred Fire.* University of Manitoba Press, 2015.

Goulet, George R.D. *The Métis: Memorable Events and Memorable Personalities.* Strong Nations, 2011.

Maracle, Lee. *Celia's Song.* Cormorant Books, 2014.

―――. *I Am Woman.* Press Gang, 2003.

―――. *Memory Serves: Oratories.* NeWest Press 2015.

Maracle, Lee, Bobb, Columpa, Carter, Tanya. *Hope Matters.* Book*hug Press, 2019.

Morin, Joshua. *Michif Language Course.* Michif Cultural Connections, St. Albert, 2021.

St-Onge, Nicole, Carolyn Podruchny, Brenda Macdougall, and Maria Campbell. *Contours of a People: Metis Family, Mobility and History.* University of Oklahoma Press, 2012.

> *I love a bibliography that rivers. When some of it rushes ahead and rapids over rocks. When some of it pools.*
> *Learn how to swim before you write a bibliography.*

Home: rivers I've learned from, rivers I've been, rivers I've lived alongside

The Red River, where my ancestors paddled and translated and fell in love and made families and became a Nation.

The North Saskatchewan. The South Saskatchewan. Morris River. Red Deer River. Bow River. Rennie's River.

All the big and little streams and rivers we gave our own names to and/or whose names we never heard.

> *Poems can be floatation devices. So can a song, new or old.*
> *Bibliographies are often written on the other side of songs. One side bibliography, the other side song.*
> *A new word learned in Michif can be a floatation device.*

Home: scholars and theories I've learned from so far

Brenda Macdougall, homeland, mobility, and relations. Jon Corbett, geo humanities and the Indigenous Geoweb. Alison Blunt, Robyn Dowling, critical geographies of home. Katherine Brickell, mapping home. Dominic Alaazi, Jeffrey Masuda, Joshua Evans and Jino Distasio. Tim Cresswell, place and mobility.

bell hooks. C Despres. A Gorman-Murray. Douglas Porteous and Sandra Smith. Doreen Massey. Steff Jansen and Staffan Löfving. Shelly Mallet.

Jennifer Adese and Chris Andersen, whose research brings me home.

Adese, Jennifer and Chris Andersen, eds. *A People and a Nation: New Directions in Contemporary Métis Studies.* UBC Press, 2021.

Alaazi, Dominic A., Jeffrey R. Masuda, Joshua Evans, and Jino Distasio. "Therapeutic Landscapes of Home: Exploring Indigenous Peoples' Experiences of a Housing First Intervention in Winnipeg." *Social Science & Medicine* 147 (December), 2015, pp. 30–37.

Andersen, Chris. *"Métis": Race, Recognition and the Struggle for Indigenous Peoplehood.* UBC Press, 2014.

Belcourt, Herb. *Walking in the Woods: A Métis Journey.* Victoria: Brindle & Glass, 2006.

Blunt, Alison. "Cultural Geographies of Migration: Mobility, Transnationality and Diaspora." *Progress in Human Geography* 31(5), 2007, pp. 684–94.

Blunt, Alison, Jayani Bonnerjee, Caron Lipman, Joanna Long, Felicity Paynter. "My Home: text, space and performance." *Cultural Geographies* 14, 2017, pp. 309–18.

Blunt, Alison, and Robyn Dowling. *Home (Key Ideas in Geography)*. Taylor & Francis, 2006.

Brickell, Katherine. "'Mapping' and 'Doing' Critical Geographies of Home." *Progress of Human Geography* 36(2), 2010, pp. 225–44.

Corbett, J. M. "'I don't come from anywhere': Exploring the role of VGI and the Geoweb in rediscovering a sense of place in a dispersed Aboriginal community." In *Crowdsourcing Geographic Knowledge: Volunteered Geographic Information (VGI) in Theory and Practice,* eds. D. Sui, M. Goodchild, & S. Elwood, 2012, pp 223–41.

Corbett, Jon, Mike Evans, Gabrielle Legault, and Zachary Romano "Relocating a Sense of Place Using the Participatory Geoweb: The Historical Document Database of the Métis Nation of British Columbia. *International Journal of Applied Geospatial Research.* 6(1), 2015, pp. 24–38.

Cresswell, Tim. "Towards a Politics of Mobility." *Environment and Planning D: Society and Space* 28(1), 2010, pp. 17–31.

Evans, M., C. Andersen, D. Dietrich, C. Bourrassa, T. Logan, L.D. Berg, and E. Devolder. "Funding and ethics in Métis community based research: The complications of a contemporary context." *International Journal of Critical Indigenous Studies*, 5(1), 2012, p. 54.

Finley, Robert, Patrick Friesen, Aislinn Hunter, Anne Simpson, and Jan Zwicky. *A Ragged Pen,* 2006.

Frank, Arthur. "Why Study People's Stories? The Dialogical Ethics of Narrative Analysis." *International Journal of Qualitative Methods* 1(1), 2002.

Gorman-Murray, A., and Robyn Dowling. "Home." *M/C* 10, no. 4, 2007.

Hall, A. J. *Earth into Property: Colonization, Decolonization, and Capitalism*. McGill-Queen's University Press, 2010.

Hancock, Brendan. "An Interview with Lee Maracle." CWILA Canadian Women In The Literary Arts. March 23, 2010.

hooks, bell. "A Place Where the Soul Can Rest." In *Belonging: A Culture of Place*, by bell hooks. Taylor & Francis, Inc, 2008.

Jansen, Steff, and Staffan Löfving. *Struggles for Home: Violence, Hope and the Movement of People*. Berghahn Books, 2008.

King, Thomas. *The Back of the Turtle*. Harper Collins, 2014.

———. *The Truth about Stories*. House of Anansi Press, 2003.

LaDuke, W. *All Our Relations: Native Struggles for Land and Life*. South End Press, 1999.

Leavy, Patricia. *Method Meets Art: Arts-Based Research Practice*. Guilford Press, 2009.

Leclair, C. Métis environmental knowledge: La tayr pi tout li moond. PhD diss., York University, 2003.

———. "Memory Alive: Race, Religion and Metis Identities." *Essays on Canadian Writing* 75, 2002, pp. 159–76.

———. "Métis Wisdom: Learning and Teaching Across the Cultures." *Atlantis: A Women's Studies Journal*, Spring, 1998, pp. 123–26.

Lundgren, Jodi. "'Being A Half-Breed' Discourses Of Race And Cultural Syncreticity In The Works Of Three Metis Women Writers." *Canadian Literature* 144, 1995. May 10, 2015.

Macdougall, Brenda. *One of the Family: Métis Culture in Nineteenth Century Northwestern Saskatchewan*. University of British Columbia Press, 2010.

Macdougall, Brenda, Carolyn Podruchny, and Nicole St-Onge, eds. "Introduction: Cultural Mobility and Contours of Difference." In *Contours of Metis Landscapes: Family, Mobility, and History in Northwestern North America*. University of Oklahoma Press, 2012.

Mallett, Shelley. "Understanding Home: A Critical Review of the Literature." *The Sociological Review* 52(1), 2004, pp. 62–89.

Massey, Doreen. "A Place Called Home." *New Formations* 17, 1992, pp. 3–15.

McLeod, Neal, ed. *Indigenous Poetics in Canada*. Wilfrid Laurier University Press, 2014.

McGuire, Patricia D. 'Wiisaakodewikwe Anishinaabekwe Diabaajimotaw Nipigon Zaaga'Igan: Lake Nipigon Ojibway Metis Stories about Women.' *Canadian Woman Studies* 26(3), 2015, pp. 217–22.

Mignolo, Walter. "Decolonizing Western Epistemology / Building Decolonial Epistemologies." *Latina/o Theology and Philosophy*, November 2011, pp. 19–43.

Mishenene, Rachel. *Strength and Struggle: Perspectives From First Nations, Inuit, and Métis Peoples in Canada*. McGraw-Hill Ryerson, 2011.

O'Brien, Susie. "'Please Eunice, Don't Be Ignorant': The White Reader As Trickster In Lee Maracle's Fiction." *Canadian Literature* 144, 1995, pp. 82-96.

Oliver, Mary. *Long Life: Essays and Other Writings*. Da Capo Press, 2005.

———. *Upstream*. Penguin Press, 2016.

Perrault, Jeanne, and Sylvia Vance. *Writing the Circle: Native Women of Western Canada*. NeWest Press, 1990.

Porteous, Douglas J., and Sandra E. Smith. *Domicide: The Global Destruction of Home*. McGill-Queen's University Press, 2001.

Rundstrom, R. A. GIS, Indigenous Peoples, and Epistemological Diversity. *Cartography and Geographic Information Systems*, 22(1), 1995, pp. 45–57.

Simpson, Leanne Betasamosake. *Islands of Decolonial Love*. ARP Books, 2013.

Smith, L. T. *Decolonizing Methodologies: Research and Indigenous Peoples*. Zed Books, 2001.

Wilson, Shawn. *Research is Ceremony: Indigenous Research Methods*. Fernwood Publishing, 2008.

Woodcock, George. "Prairie Writers and the Métis: Rudy Wiebe and Margaret Laurence." *Canadian Ethnic Studies* 14(1), 1982, pp. 9–22.

That story your grandmother told late into the night when you were fourteen can be a floatation device, too.

Your grandfather's woodpile or your grandfather's fiddle can be your bibliography, keep your head above water.

Home: land I've learned from, places I've lived

Winnipeg, where they performed. St. Albert. Mission, where so many of my mother's stories took place. Calgary. Edmonton. Wetaskiwin. Baker. Christine Meikle School. Sturgeon River Apartments. Lion's Park. The train tracks. Claresholm. ▮▮▮ Ranch.
Saint John and St. John's. St. Albert. Alberta. Treaty 1 territory in Manitoba, the heart of the Métis Nation.

A bibliography speaks around the story.
A bibliography is too long and too short at the same time.
A bibliography avoids criticism.
A bibliography stops before it gets to the good life.

Métis scholars, researchers and teachers I've learned from so far

Jean Teillet. Christine Welsh. Maria Campbell, again and again. Kim Anderson. Robert Hancock. Daniel Voth. Robert Alexander Innes. June Scudeler. Paul Gareau. Adam Gaudry. Herb Belcourt. Toni Culjak. Kristina Fagan. Marsii.

Adese, Jennifer. "Restoring the Balance: Métis Women and Contemporary Nationalist Political Organizing." In Jennifer Adese and Chris Andersen, eds. *A People and a Nation: New Directions in Contemporary Métis Studies,* UBC Press, 2021, pp. 115–45.

Andersen, Chris. "Peoplehood and the Nation Form: Core Concepts for a Critical Métis Studies." In Jennifer Adese and Chris Andersen, eds. *A People and a Nation: New Directions in Contemporary Métis Studies,* UBC Press, 2021, pp. 18–39.

Anderson, Kim, and Maria Campbell. *Life Stages and Native Women: Memory, Teachings and Story Medicine.* University of Manitoba Press, 2012.

Campbell, Maria. *Stories of the Road Allowance People.* The Gabriel Dumont Institute, 2010.

Culjak, Toni A. "Searching For A Place In Between: The Autobiographies Of Three Canadian Métis Women." *American Review of Canadian Studies* 31(1–2), 2010, pp. 137–57.

Fagan, Kristina. "'Well done old half breed woman': Lydia Campbell and the Labrador Literary Tradition." *Papers Of The Bibliographical Society Of Canada/Cahiers De La Société Bibliographique Du Canada* 48(1), 2010, pp. 49–76.

Gareau, Paul L. "Mary and the Métis: Religion as a Site for New Insight in Métis Studies." In Jennifer Adese and Chris Andersen, eds. *A People and a Nation: New Directions in Contemporary Métis Studies,* UBC Press, 2021, pp. 188–212.

Gaudry, Adam. "Building the Field of Métis Studies: Toward Transformative and Empowering Métis Scholarship." In Jennifer Adese and Chris Andersen, eds. *A People and a Nation: New Directions in Contemporary Métis Studies,* UBC Press, 2021, pp. 213–29.

Hancock, Robert. "The Power of Peoplehood: Reimagining Métis Relationships, Research, and Responsibilities." In

Jennifer Adese and Chris Andersen, eds. *A People and a Nation: New Directions in Contemporary Métis Studies,* UBC Press, 2021, pp. 40–66.

Innes, Robert Alexander. "Challenging a Racist Fiction: A Closer Look at Métis-First Nations Relations." In Jennifer Adese and Chris Andersen, eds. *A People and a Nation: New Directions in Contemporary Métis Studies,* UBC Press, 2021, pp. 92–114.

Scudeler, June. "We're Still Here and Still Métis: Rewriting the 1885 Resistance in Marilyn Dumont's *The Pemmican Eaters.*" In Jennifer Adese and Chris Andersen, eds. *A People and a Nation: New Directions in Contemporary Métis Studies,* UBC Press, 2021, pp. 170–87.

Teillet, Jean. *The North-West Is Our Mother: The Story of Louis Riel's People, the Métis Nation.* Harper Collins, 2021.

Thistle, Jesse. "Alcide Morrisette: Oral Histories of a Métis Man on the Prairies in the Mid-Twentieth Century." In Jennifer Adese and Chris Andersen, eds. *A People and a Nation: New Directions in Contemporary Métis Studies,* UBC Press, 2021, pp. 146–69.

Voth, Daniel. "The Race Question in Canada and the Politics of Racial Mixing." In Jennifer Adese and Chris Andersen, eds. *A People and a Nation: New Directions in Contemporary Métis Studies,* UBC Press, 2021, pp. 67–91.

Welsh, Christine. "Voices of the Grandmothers: Reclaiming a Métis Heritage." *Canadian Literature* 131, 1991, pp. 15–24.

This bibliography changes shape each time you look at it.

A bibliography should be transported only by canoe or kayak. The spray will make it damp and let the story on the other side leak through.

A bibliography should be prepared like pemmican.

Home: land I've learned from, places I've lived

That raspberry patch in the backwoods of British Columbia. Auntie Janice's land and all the food she made for us. Auntie Bev's backyard. The Saskatoon bushes we found in the woods in St. Albert. Batoche.

Vis Island. The salty ocean where I swam and knew where I was.

The blueberry patches on the edge here in Newfoundland and Labrador. The oceanside cliffs that make me think of the grassland back home. All the bison returning to the Prairies after a century of struggle. You are so brave. All my relations.

This bibliography will grow.

I want you all to know that I've read more than this and I will read more than this.

I've lived more stories than these. I will live more.

Beneath my skin are the bones of stories.

A story is the best kind of bibliography.

Everything is related. The end is related to the beginning and everything is related to the middle.

Now, you tell me.

Books in the Life Writing Series
Published by Wilfrid Laurier University Press

Haven't Any News: Ruby's Letters from the Fifties edited by Edna Staebler with an Afterword by Marlene Kadar • 1995 / x + 172 pp. / ISBN 978-0-88920-248-1

"I Want to Join Your Club": Letters from Rural Children, 1900–1920 edited by Norah L. Lewis with a Preface by Neil Sutherland • 1996 / xii + 250 pp. (30 b&w photos) / ISBN 978-0-88920-260-3

And Peace Never Came by Elisabeth M. Raab with Historical Notes by Marlene Kadar • 1996 / x + 196 pp. (12 b&w photos, map) / ISBN 978-0-88920-292-4

Dear Editor and Friends: Letters from Rural Women of the North-West, 1900–1920 edited by Norah L. Lewis • 1998 / xvi + 166 pp. (20 b&w photos) / ISBN 978-0-88920-287-0

The Surprise of My Life: An Autobiography by Claire Drainie Taylor with a Foreword by Marlene Kadar • 1998 / xii + 268 pp. (8 colour photos and 92 b&w photos) / ISBN 978-0-88920-302-0

Memoirs from Away: A New Found Land Girlhood by Helen M. Buss / Margaret Clarke • 1998 / xvi + 154 pp. / ISBN 978-0-88920-350-1

The Life and Letters of Annie Leake Tuttle: Working for the Best by Marilyn Färdig Whiteley • 1999 / xviii + 150 pp. / ISBN 978-0-88920-330-3

Marian Engel's Notebooks: "Ah, mon cahier, écoute" edited by Christl Verduyn • 1999 / viii + 576 pp. / ISBN 978-0-88920-333-4 cloth / ISBN 978-0-88920-349-5 paper

Be Good, Sweet Maid: The Trials of Dorothy Joudrie by Audrey Andrews • 1999 / vi + 276 pp. / ISBN 978-0-88920-334-1

Working in Women's Archives: Researching Women's Private Literature and Archival Documents edited by Helen M. Buss and Marlene Kadar • 2001 / vi + 120 pp. / ISBN 978-0-88920-341-9

Repossessing the World: Reading Memoirs by Contemporary Women by Helen M. Buss • 2002 / xxvi + 206 pp. / ISBN 978-0-88920-408-9 cloth / ISBN 978-0-88920-409-6 paper

Chasing the Comet: A Scottish-Canadian Life by Patricia Koretchuk • 2002 / xx + 244 pp. / ISBN 978-0-88920-407-2

The Queen of Peace Room by Magie Dominic • 2002 / xiv + 114 pp. / ISBN 978-0-88920-417-1

China Diary: The Life of Mary Austin Endicott by Shirley Jane Endicott • 2002 / xvi + 254 pp. / ISBN 978-0-88920-412-6

The Curtain: Witness and Memory in Wartime Holland by Henry G. Schogt • 2003 / xii + 132 pp. / ISBN 978-0-88920-396-9

Teaching Places by Audrey J. Whitson • 2003 / xiv + 182 pp. (9 colour photos) / ISBN 978-0-88920-425-6

Through the Hitler Line by Laurence F. Wilmot, M.C. • 2003 / xvi + 152 pp. / ISBN 978-0-88920-426-3 cloth / ISBN 978-0-88920-448-5 paper

Where I Come From by Vijay Agnew • 2003 / xiv + 298 pp. / ISBN 978-0-88920-414-0

The Water Lily Pond by Han Z. Li • 2004 / x + 254 pp. / ISBN 978-0-88920-431-7

The Life Writings of Mary Baker McQuesten: Victorian Matriarch edited by Mary J. Anderson • 2004 / xxii + 338 pp. / ISBN 978-0-88920-437-9

Seven Eggs Today: The Diaries of Mary Armstrong, 1859 and 1869 edited by Jackson W. Armstrong • 2004 / xvi + 228 pp. / ISBN 978-0-88920-440-9 cloth / ISBN 978-0-55458-439-0 paper

Love and War in London: A Woman's Diary 1939–1942 by Olivia Cockett; edited by Robert W. Malcolmson • 2005 / xvi + 208 pp. / ISBN 978-0-88920-458-4

Incorrigible by Velma Demerson • 2004 / vi + 178 pp. / ISBN 978-0-88920-444-7

Auto/biography in Canada: Critical Directions edited by Julie Rak • 2005 / viii + 264 pp. / ISBN 978-0-88920-478-2

Tracing the Autobiographical edited by Marlene Kadar, Linda Warley, Jeanne Perreault, and Susanna Egan • 2005 / viii + 280 pp. / ISBN 978-0-88920-476-8

Must Write: Edna Staebler's Diaries edited by Christl Verduyn • 2005 / viii + 304 pp. / ISBN 978-0-88920-481-2

Pursuing Giraffe: A 1950s Adventure by Anne Innis Dagg • 2006 / xvi + 284 pp. (46 b&w photos, 2 maps) / 978-0-88920-463-8

Food That Really Schmecks by Edna Staebler • 2007 / xxiv + 334 pp. / ISBN 978-0-88920-521-5

163256: A Memoir of Resistance by Michael Englishman • 2007 / xvi + 112 pp. (14 b&w photos) / ISBN 978-1-55458-009-5

The Wartime Letters of Leslie and Cecil Frost, 1915–1919 edited by R.B. Fleming • 2007 / xxxvi + 384 pp. (49 b&w photos, 5 maps) / ISBN 978-1-55458-000-2 cloth / ISBN 978-1-55458-470-3 paper

Johanna Krause Twice Persecuted: Surviving in Nazi Germany and Communist East Germany by Carolyn Gammon and Christiane Hemker • 2007 / x + 170 pp. (58 b&w photos, 2 maps) / ISBN 978-1-55458-006-4

Watermelon Syrup: A Novel by Annie Jacobsen with Jane Finlay-Young and Di Brandt • 2007 / x + 268 pp. / ISBN 978-1-55458-005-7

Broad Is the Way: Stories from Mayerthorpe by Margaret Norquay • 2008 / x + 106 pp. (6 b&w photos) / ISBN 978-1-55458-020-0

Becoming My Mother's Daughter: A Story of Survival and Renewal by Erika Gottlieb • 2008 / x + 178 pp. (36 b&w illus., 17 colour) / ISBN 978-1-55458-030-9

Leaving Fundamentalism: Personal Stories edited by G. Elijah Dann • 2008 / xii + 234 pp. / ISBN 978-1-55458-026-2

Bearing Witness: Living with Ovarian Cancer edited by Kathryn Carter and Lauri Elit • 2009 / viii + 94 pp. / ISBN 978-1-55458-055-2

Dead Woman Pickney: A Memoir of Childhood in Jamaica by Yvonne Shorter Brown • 2010 / viii + 202 pp. / ISBN 978-1-55458-189-4

I Have a Story to Tell You by Seemah C. Berson • 2010 / xx + 288 pp. (24 b&w photos) / ISBN 978-1-55458-219-8

We All Giggled: A Bourgeois Family Memoir by Thomas O. Hueglin • 2010 / xiv + 232 pp. (20 b&w photos) / ISBN 978-1-55458-262-4

Just a Larger Family: Letters of Marie Williamson from the Canadian Home Front, 1940–1944 edited by Mary F. Williamson and Tom Sharp • 2011 / xxiv + 378 pp. (16 b&w photos) / ISBN 978-1-55458-323-2

Burdens of Proof: Faith, Doubt, and Identity in Autobiography by Susanna Egan • 2011 / x + 200 pp. / ISBN 978-1-55458-333-1

Accident of Fate: A Personal Account 1938–1945 by Imre Rochlitz with Joseph Rochlitz • 2011 / xiv + 226 pp. (50 b&w photos, 5 maps) / ISBN 978-1-55458-267-9

The Green Sofa by Natascha Würzbach, translated by Raleigh Whitinger • 2012 / xiv + 240 pp. (5 b&w photos) / ISBN 978-1-55458-334-8

Unheard Of: Memoirs of a Canadian Composer by John Beckwith • 2012 / x + 393 pp. (74 illus., 8 musical examples) / ISBN 978-1-55458-358-4

Borrowed Tongues: Life Writing, Migration, and Translation by Eva C. Karpinski • 2012 / viii + 274 pp. / ISBN 978-1-55458-357-7

Basements and Attics, Closets and Cyberspace: Explorations in Canadian Women's Archives edited by Linda M. Morra and Jessica Schagerl • 2012 / x + 338 pp. / ISBN 978-1-55458-632-5

The Memory of Water by Allen Smutylo • 2013 / x + 262 pp. (65 colour illus.) / ISBN 978-1-55458-842-8

The Unwritten Diary of Israel Unger, Revised Edition by Carolyn Gammon and Israel Unger • 2013 / x + 230 pp. (90 b&w illus.) / ISBN 978-1-77112-011-1

Boom! Manufacturing Memoir for the Popular Market by Julie Rak • 2013 / viii + 250 pp. (7 b&w illus.) / ISBN 978-1-55458-939-5

Motherlode: A Mosaic of Dutch Wartime Experience by Carolyne Van Der Meer • 2014 / xiv + 132 pp. (6 b&w illus.) / ISBN 978-1-77112-005-0

Not the Whole Story: Challenging the Single Mother Narrative edited by Lea Caragata and Judit Alcalde • 2014 / x + 222 pp. / ISBN 978-1-55458-624-0

Street Angel by Magie Dominic • 2014 / vii + 154 pp. / ISBN 978-1-77112-026-5

In the Unlikeliest of Places: How Nachman Libeskind Survived the Nazis, Gulags, and Soviet Communism by Annette Libeskind Berkovits • 2014 / xiv + 282 pp. (6 colour illus.) / ISBN 978-1-77112-066-1

Kinds of Winter: Four Solo Journeys by Dogteam in Canada's Northwest Territories by Dave Olesen • 2014 / xii + 256 pp. (17 b&w illus., 6 maps) / ISBN 978-1-77112-118-7

Working Memory: Women and Work in World War II edited by Marlene Kadar and Jeanne Perreault • 2015 / viii + 246 pp. (46 b&w and colour illus.) / ISBN 978-1-77112-035-7

Wait Time: A Memoir of Cancer by Kenneth Sherman • 2016 / xiv + 138 pp. / ISBN 978-1-77112-188-0

Canadian Graphic: Picturing Life Narratives edited by Candida Rifkind and Linda Warley • 2016 / viii + 310 pp. (59 colour and b&w illus.) / ISBN 978-1-77112-179-8

Travels and Identities: Elizabeth and Adam Shortt in Europe, 1911 edited by Peter E. Paul Dembski • 2017 / xxii + 272 pp. (9 b&w illus.) / ISBN 978-1-77112-225-2

Bird-Bent Grass: A Memoir, in Pieces by Kathleen Venema • 2018 • viii + 346 pp. / ISBN 978-1-77112-290-0

My Basilian Priesthood, 1961–1967 by Michael Quealey • 2019 • viii + 222 pp. / ISBN 978-1-77112-242-9

What the Oceans Remember: Searching for Belonging and Home by Sonja Boon • 2019 • xvi + 320 pp. (8 b&w illus.) / ISBN 978-1-77112-423-2

Rough and Plenty: A Memorial by Raymond A. Rogers • 2020 • x + 316 pp. (9 b&w photos) / ISBN 978-1-77112-436-2

Limelight: Canadian Women and the Rise of Celebrity Autobiography by Katja Lee • 2020 • viii + 360 pp. (6 colour images) / ISBN 978-1-77112-429-4

Prison Life Writing: Conversion and the Literary Roots of the U.S. Prison System by Simon Rolston • 2021 • x + 316 pp. / ISBN 1-77112-517-8

Scratching River by Michelle Porter • 2022 • xiv + 168 pp. / ISBN 978-1-77112-544-4